THE BIG WHISTLE

THE
BIG
WHISTLE

Bill Chadwick
with Hal Bock

An Associated Features Book

HAWTHORN BOOKS, INC.
PUBLISHERS/*New York*

For Millie,
who made it all possible

CONTENTS

ACKNOWLEDGMENTS

Gilbert and Sullivan, in *The Pirates of Penzance,* wrote, "When constabulary duty's to be done . . . a policeman's lot is not a happy one." Well, my 16 years as a National Hockey League "policeman" were full of happy memories because of people like Tommy Lockhart, Frank Calder, King Clancy, Clarence Campbell, and countless others. Afterward, this arm of the law moved to the broadcast booth thanks to Emile Francis and the New York Ranger organization and received considerable help from pros like Marv Albert, Sal Marchiano, and Jim Gordon. I want to acknowledge them all.

Bill Chadwick

Telling another man's story is no easy task, unless the other man is Bill Chadwick. He made it easy and so did my personal referee, Fran, and goaltender, Richie, who, in fact, make everything easy for me.

Hal Bock

THE
BIG
WHISTLE

PROLOGUE

I never saw the puck.

It was as simple as that. I was looking down at the ice, stepping over the hockey dasher boards on the Fiftieth Street side of Madison Square Garden in New York City and being careful not to get my skates tangled up. I didn't want to land on my nose. I wouldn't have looked like much of a hockey player if I had tripped the moment I stepped on the ice.

I remember stopping at the edge of the rink and looking out at the ice, thinking how good it would feel to step out there and glide away. I knew my dad was in the stands, watching, and I didn't want to embarrass him by flopping. That's why my head was bent and my eyes were transfixed on the gray-colored ice as I stepped from the rubber runner over the dasher boards.

That's why I never saw that damned puck.

I had been playing in the Metropolitan Junior Hockey League for the New York Stock Exchange team. I would work in the Exchange during the day and then play hockey at night. The pay was $15 per week, and it had to be the best job in the whole world. I would be on the floor of the Exchange from ten until three, working as a page boy. My main job, really, was to represent them playing hockey, and imagine getting paid $15 a week—which was big money in 1935—to work only 20 hours a week and spend the rest of your time playing hockey. How could you beat that?

I was a center, and I became the best player the Stock Exchange had. I won the Met League scoring championship, and that's how I happened to be on the team of the Met League Junior All-Stars selected to play a team of all-stars from the Boston area.

Our team dressed in the Garden locker room next door to the one used by the old New York Americans. There was a surge of excitement churning through my body as I strapped on my shin guards and laced my skates. Imagine, Buster Chadwick, a kid born on 122nd Street and Second Avenue in Manhattan, playing hockey in Madison Square Garden, on an all-star team. It was a great feeling.

The Boston team was already on the ice when we left our dressing room. They were warming up at one end of the Garden rink, skating around casually, passing a couple of pucks among themselves. In a few moments, we would be doing the same thing at the other end. Then the goalies would slip into the nets and we'd line up for a more formal warmup. I remember thinking about what shots I'd try in the warmup. Aim for the corners, I told myself. It was the last thing I thought of as I hit the ice.

At that precise moment one of the Boston players shot a puck high, and I was on a collision course with that frozen hunk of rubber. There was no time to duck or even flinch. It happened that fast. The puck crashed right into my face, hitting me above my right eye. I can still remember the surge of pain tearing through my eye and reaching, it seemed, deep into my brain. It felt as if someone had poked me in the eye with a soldering iron.

I fell to the ice, clutching at my face with my hands, as if trying to tear that awful, throbbing pain out of my eye, and I was spilling blood over that clean ice surface as they carted me off to the Garden's medical office.

The Madison Square Garden physician was Dr. Henry Klaus, who spent a good deal of his time across the street from the Garden in a local bar. He had a better elbow than Sandy Koufax, if you ask me. Anyway, Dr. Klaus stitched up the cut and sent me to Manhattan Eye and Ear Hospital to see what further damage had been done to the eye. My dad went with me, and I can remember him trying to encourage me not to worry. But he had a look on his face that told me he was plenty worried.

They bedded me down in the hospital and I spent a week there, undergoing all kinds of tests. Doctors would come and go, in and out, shining lights in my eye and wiggling their fingers in front of my face, telling me to look this way and that. My eye was black, but that didn't bother me because I wasn't worried about my looks. What did concern me was that expression on pop's face every time he came to visit and the grim look of the doctors every time they examined me.

While I was on my back in the hospital, my teammates weren't exactly wiped out by my absence. They beat that Boston team and continued on to the national tournament. They finished second and received handsome medals for the achievement. Even though I never got two feet out onto the ice for them in that playoff, I was so proud of them I could have busted. I was part and parcel of that team, and when they gave out those second-place medals, the guys got one for me, too. That medal tickled the daylights out of me, for at that time I really needed something to lift my spirits.

I realized something was wrong because of all the whispering and head-shaking that was going on in that hospital. And I knew from the expressions on everybody's faces that when they got around to giving their patient the news, it wasn't going to be good.

I was a terrible-looking sight. Half of my face was a different color than the other half and my eye was still swollen shut. Mom and pop would come to see me every day to keep up my spirits, but the only thing that would cheer me was for the doctors to take the wraps off that eye. Each day seemed to drag for me until the moment of truth arrived.

Finally, the doctors indicated they were ready to let me know the story once and for all. They came into my room, and I carefully prepared myself for anything they might say.

"We've got good news, Bill," one of them began. "You'll be going home tomorrow."

"Great!" I shouted. "Hey, dad, isn't that great?" I said to my father, who was at my bedside. "I'm finally getting out of here."

But pop wasn't excited. He seemed just as grim as he had been the week before when he brought me into the hospital from the Garden. Something was wrong, and he knew it.

"There's something else, Bill," the doctor continued. He looked me straight in the face, and at that moment I felt almost like a mind reader. I knew what he was going to say next, and my body shuddered ever so slightly as the words cut into me, each one burning me every bit as painfully as that shot to the eye had a week earlier.

"We can't save your eye, Bill," said the doctor. "It's gone. You'll never have any central vision in it for the rest of your life."

1
POP GETS HIS DANDER UP

There were no pucks around when I first learned to skate. That's because there wasn't any ice in Manhattan either, where I grew up. But ask any kid who lives in the city about roller-skating and he'll tell you it's the next best thing to the ice variety. I did my share of it, too, skating all around the streets with my friends.

Pop wasn't a wealthy man. He drove a team of horses for the Bauer Trucking Company in the city and later drove a truck for them. He was also a stonemason, and that was a funny kind of job . You couldn't work in the rain or when the temperature dropped below 40 degrees. And if you couldn't work, you didn't get paid. So, everything depended on the weather. When pop worked, he made good money. When he didn't, it was soup the next day.

With money scarce, there wasn't a lot of room for frills in our family. So I had roller skates, but not ice skates. I remember one time when I was about nine years old. One of my cousins came over to visit. "Hey, Buster," he said, "let's go skating up in Van Cortlandt Park."

"Nah," I answered, brushing off the suggestion. "I can't ice-skate, and besides, all I have are roller skates."

"C'mon," he insisted. "If you can roller-skate, you can

ice-skate. I've got my skates and you can share them with me."

Because I couldn't answer his logical arguments, I agreed to go off with him. We got up to the park early. It wasn't too crowded, so when I fell down, I wasn't embarrassed.

My cousin had a pair of clamp-on skates and we took turns using them. First, he'd skate for awhile. Then, when he got winded, he'd take the skates off and I'd put them on. While he rested, I skated. Then, we switched again. The system worked out so well that we did it again for the next two days in Central Park. I'll never forget those three days, because that marked the first time for me on ice skates. Surprisingly, I didn't break my neck. In fact, I had a good time. My cousin, I discovered, was right. If you could roller-skate, you could ice-skate.

At about that time my family moved from Manhattan to Jamaica, Queens. Today, Jamaica is just another section of New York City, but in those days it was the suburbs, a countrified area that barely resembled Manhattan. It even had ice, a fact I discovered fast. Down at Baisley Park the lake froze early in the winters, and you could skate to your heart's content. The one thing you needed, though, was skates. Pop took care of that problem.

My father was great about things like that. We could never be mistaken for a wealthy family, and in fact, we had very, very little money. But pop was always behind me as far as anything I wanted to do in sports. Somehow, when he found out that I liked to skate, he came up with a pair of skates for me.

They were racing skates, quite the popular thing in those days with the new Silver Skate Tournament getting under way. One of the Silver Skate champions was Irving Jaffee, and he became a hero for me, because he also was a native New Yorker. Jaffee went on to win Olympic gold medals in speed-skating.

At Jamaica High School I played freshman baseball, and after school, I'd go over to Baisley Park with my racing skates and play ice hockey. I was good at baseball, but I was even better at ice hockey. So, when I reached my second year of high school, I decided to lend my newly found hockey expertise to the school team. I discovered in a hurry that the players weren't exactly anxious to have me.

First of all, you have to understand that the hockey players at Jamaica were the elite of the school. They were the "in" crowd and were in no particular hurry to let me into their group. After all, I was from the other side of the tracks—Baisley Park. The Jamaica hockey players all came from another section and played at Goose Pond, about five miles away. I'd hop a bus to get over there but they never greeted me with open arms. Finally, I decided that I could beat those guys at their own game. I asked for a tryout.

"Sure," they told me. "You can try out. Be at our next practice."

"Where's that?" I asked.

"The Brooklyn Ice Palace," came the casual reply.

The Ice Palace was a public rink in downtown Brooklyn. To get there from Jamaica, you had to take a bus to the Long Island Rail Road and then take a train to Brooklyn. The practice started at six o'clock in the morning and afterwards, we had to rush out of there, hop back on the LIRR and bus and be back in Jamaica for an 8:00 A.M. class. It was no easy trip, but if I wanted to make the team, that was what I'd have to do.

The day of my tryout was cold and windy, and the trip in the drafty LIRR was no picnic. I had my racing skates slung over my shoulder and hurried through the streets to the Ice Palace, where many of the Jamaica players were already skating.

I rushed to the benches and started slipping on my skates. I tightened them quickly, and I could feel my pulse quicken as

I stepped out on the ice. Just then, I heard the voice behind me. It was shrill and sounded urgent.

"Hey, you! Whitey! Get over here."

I knew they wanted me because most of the other players were staring at the new guy with the blond hair. I glided over to the sideboards to find out what was up.

"You can't play hockey in those things," said the voice, less urgent now but still stern. "Those are racing skates. They're not allowed. Get off the ice."

"But they're the only skates I've got," I said, protesting.

I might as well have been talking to the wall. "Get off the ice!" came the answer, this time more urgently.

So Chadwick tiptoed his way back to the bench, trying not to look as foolish as he felt. I sat down next to one of my best friends, Charlie Campbell. At five feet, six inches, Charlie was five inches shorter than I was. He glanced at me and saw that I was really peeved.

"What's wrong?" asked Campbell.

"These damned skates," I snapped. "They won't let me try out with them."

"No problem," said Charlie. "Here, wear mine."

It was a nice idea, but Charlie's foot wasn't nearly as big as mine. How could I squeeze my size 11 foot into his size 9 skates? The answer was: not easily.

I pushed and Charlie tugged and eventually I was into his skates. It wasn't the most comfortable fit in the world, I can tell you, but they were hockey skates and that was all that mattered at that particular moment. I hopped over the boards, and this time nobody chased me off the ice.

After coming so close to washing out, I skated like the wind. I went up and down that ice as if Charlie Campbell's skates had motors in them. I had made up my mind that I was going to make this team.

We practiced for an hour or so, and when it was over, Buster Chadwick was a full-fledged member of Jamaica High

School's hockey team. I was proud as a peacock about it, too. To play in the Public Schools Athletic League (PSAL) you needed a signed permission slip from your parents. I grabbed the form and made a beeline back to the LIRR for the trip to Queens and morning classes. That evening I told pop what had happened.

I was an only child, and because of that my mother was very protective. She worried when I went down to the corner for a loaf of bread. Getting her permission to play for Jamaica was going to be no simple job, and both dad and I knew it. Together we tried to dream up a strategic plan to win my mother's approval, but one idea after another seemed doomed to failure.

Finally, pop stood up. "Buster," he said, "let me handle this."

Mom had already turned down football, so I figured hockey didn't stand much of a chance with her. However, there was one thing going for me. She had never seen the game and didn't know much about it. And I knew that dad could be pretty persuasive. I listened at the doorway as he brought up the subject.

"Buster brought home this slip for us to sign," he said, very matter-of-factly. That's it, pop, I thought, be casual.

Mom picked up the form and looked it over. "Hmm," she said. "Hockey. Matt, what's hockey?"

"Oh, it's skating," replied my father, staying very cool. "It's good exercise for Buster."

"Okay," said mom.

It was as simple as that. Okay. I ran into the room and hugged my mother and father. I was just tickled. And I know she was pleased that her approval had made me so excited. But I'm afraid if she had known a little more about the sport, she might not have been so pleased.

Jamaica and all of the other city schools playing hockey held their games at the Brooklyn Ice Palace. It was a weird kind of rink with sideboards running parallel on each side of the ice from the blue line. From the blue lines to the goals the ice surface widened out, but there were two obstructing poles in the middle of the ice so each team that played had two extra defensemen. And believe me, the way we played hockey, those two poles were every bit as good as our regular defensemen.

When the season began, there were all kinds of excitement in our house. I was just a bench-warmer, but it was a big event anyway. Pop drove me to the rink and mom came along for her first look at a hockey game. When she saw what I was into, she gave pop hell all the way home.

One of my teammates that first season at Jamaica was John Mitchell, who later became Attorney General of the United States under President Nixon. I also played with Mitchell later when he was going to Fordham University, and I was still at Jamaica. Now you might wonder how that happened. Well, it was simple. I was so hungry for hockey that playing for one team wasn't enough for me. I played for three at the same time.

At Jamaica I played under my own name. The PSAL would have frowned on the idea of my also playing for Fordham at the same time, so I just changed my name. When I played for the university, I used the name O'Donoghue. He was listed on the roster and had a matriculation card. But when it came to games, he stayed home and I played in his place.

When I wasn't playing for my high school or for Fordham University, I played for the Jamaica Hawks of the Metropolitan League. They played in Madison Square Garden, which was a step up from the Brooklyn Ice Palace, where we held our high school games, and the Bronx Coliseum, where Fordham played its games. With the Hawks, I used the name Flanagan. Mitchell played with me on that team, too.

I couldn't get enough hockey, and when the season ended, I spent the summer months playing catch with a puck in the streets. I'd get a kid to stand across the street and I'd shoot pucks to him all summer, dodging automobiles and becoming a better and better shooter. I made up my mind then and there that I would one day play in the National Hockey League.

But hockey wasn't the only sport for me. I also played baseball at Jamaica, and in 1933 our team went all the way to the city championship game. The title game was against George Washington High School in Ebbets Field, and you can imagine how excited we were to be playing on a major league field. Our guys were really up for the game, but we wouldn't have been if we had looked up at the sky. It was dark and ominous-looking. There were rain clouds hovering over Brooklyn as we came to bat in the first inning.

A couple of hits, a couple of walks, an error here, a wild pitch there, and all of a sudden, we had six runs on the scoreboard. Our guys on the bench were hollering and cheering like crazy, right up until the rain began to fall. It was a torrential downpour, and after an hour's delay, the umpires came into our dugout and gave us the bad news. The game had been rained out, and with it went our six-run lead.

The news was a heavy blow to us. We had fought tooth and nail to get to the championship game. We had beaten teams like Richmond Hill, which had a pretty good infielder named Phil Rizzuto, and Tilden High, which had a slugger named Sid Gordon. Both Rizzuto and Gordon went on to the major leagues. Now we gang up on Washington for six runs in the first inning of the championship game. That's like money in the bank with our best pitcher, Ken Norton, on the mound. And *poof,* the whole thing is gone because of a cloudburst. Now we'd have to play them again and do it all over again. But what were the chances of that happening again—scoring half a dozen runs in our first time at bat? I'd say that we had two chances of repeating that feat—slim and none.

Slim came through.

A week later we played George Washington again, this time at Yankee Stadium. And what do you know? Our first time at bat and the same thing happened. It was just like Ebbets Field all over again. A hit here, an error there, a couple of walks, and other good things and we had six runs on the scoreboard in the first inning again.

This time when we looked up at the sky, the sun was shining. So were we when the ball game was over and Jamaica High School had won the city championship. The final score was 15-6 and Norton, who later became athletic director at Manhattan College, needed all the runs we could get him that day.

Championships in interscholastic sports were nothing new for Jamaica High School. Over a span of 14 years the school lost only one public school hockey championship. That was in 1933 when I was captain of the hockey team. I was the only veteran back from the previous year's city champions and we almost repeated, but Brooklyn Tech beat us, 2-1, with a goal in the last period of the last game.

The referee for that game and, in fact, almost all of the PSAL games played in those days was a Brooklyn high school teacher named Harry Kane. He was a totally dedicated man and he knew how to handle wise-guy loudmouths like the captain of the Jamaica team. I felt I had to carry our team, and I crabbed and complained every time the referee made a call against us. I was so wrapped up in the game that I believed every decision that went against Jamaica had to be wrong. Those sound-off sessions often ended with Harry Kane directing me to the penalty box. I wasn't a dirty player, but I was hard-nosed and I gave as much as I got. I wasn't exactly subtle about it either.

Jamaica High School's hockey coach was Henry J. Silverman, who was an assistant principal at the school and in charge of all athletics. Like many high-school teachers, coach Silverman ran a summer camp, and in my junior year at Jamaica, he invited me to come up to his camp as a counselor.

I wasn't going to be paid because I was younger than half

of the campers at Arrowhead in Poultney, Vermont, but it was a chance to get away from the city and play ball all summer. And it was a chance to stay close to Henry J. Silverman, who had more to do with my athletic development than anybody else except my father. The coach kept me on the straight and narrow and always encouraged me to continue playing hockey.

One of the boys in my bunk at Camp Arrowhead was Dickie Baron, and in the summer of 1933, after I had graduated from Jamaica High School, his father offered me a job with the Royal Card and Paper Company. The company was located on Twenty-fifth Street and Eleventh Avenue, and I would be paid the magnificent salary of $12 a week.

Now $12 may not sound like a lot of money, but in 1933, after the stock market had crashed and the country was tossed into the lap of one gigantic depression, $12 a week wasn't half bad. I yearned to go to college, but I never did get the opportunity, because $12 a week was mighty important to our family. I split my salary democratically. I gave $10 to my folks to help with expenses at home and kept $2 for my traveling expenses and lunches. And to show how times have changed, that $2 was more than enough each week. Today, it wouldn't be enough for lunch alone for one day.

While working at Royal Card and Paper Company, I continued my involvement in sports. I played baseball in the Queens Alliance, a sort of semipro league. I wasn't bad either, although I guess, to be honest, I'd have to describe myself as "good field-no hit." I also played hockey for an outfit called the Floral Park Hockey Club. Our team was made up mostly of fellows just out of high school, and we played against other area teams.

One of those teams was the New York Stock Exchange, which also played in the Metropolitan Hockey League. Times haven't changed all that much. Today top prospects are scouted and wined and dined by the opposing professional leagues. In the 1930s the Stock Exchange team wooed me.

"How would you like to play with us?" asked Pete Baldwin, one of the Stock Exchange players and the brother of a New York City councilman.

I told him I'd love to since the Met League meant a step up in class. But there was one problem. I didn't work for the stock exchange. I was still with the paper company.

"No problem," said Baldwin. "What are you making with the paper company?"

"Twelve dollars," I said.

"Okay, I'll pay you $15."

Now if $12 was a lot of money to be earning, imagine how much an instant raise to $15 would mean. Pete Baldwin had a seat on the Exchange, and I was to be his personal page, running for the messages each time his number flashed. The work was easy, the hours ideal, the pay high, and best of all, my main function was playing hockey.

"I'll take it," I told Baldwin.

With that simple sentence, my life turned an important corner. Hockey began to assume a significant role in my life. Playing for the Stock Exchange team meant more ice time than I'd ever had before. And just as he had throughout my high school playing days, dad would be at every game we played. We played our games as prelims to the New York Rover games in Madison Square Garden each Sunday.

There was one game I will never forget. We were matched against the Van Cortlandt Broncos, and they were beating us, 3-0, which didn't do too much for my temper. Anyway, I was in front of the Van Cortlandt net trying to screen their goalie and hoping to deflect a shot past him when I felt a sharp rap across the ankle. I ignored the first one but not the second. This time I whirled on the goalie, Mickey Adelson, and we started swapping punches.

Adelson got the best of me, I must admit. I wound up with a split lip and a five-minute major penalty. He only got two minutes in the penalty box. At that time goalies had to serve their own penalties, so Adelson was in the penalty box with me and we were both still muttering at each other when I noticed a commotion behind us.

I turned around just in time to see my father, glasses and all, burst through the last cop and land one swell haymaker on Adelson. "Son," he shouted, "if you can't lick him, I will."

The next day's New York *World-Telegram* carried the story with a delightful headline that read "ICER'S POP GETS HIS DANDER UP." I cut it out and I've saved the thing to remind me of the kind of pop this icer had.

My days in the Met League are full of fond memories, and my dad shared all of them with me. He thrilled with me at my successes and sympathized with me at my failures. And having him with me helped ease the shock the day the doctors told me I'd never again see out of my right eye.

2
WHERE'S THE WHISTLE?

The doctors explained to me that the healing process of
the injury to my eye had caused a scar to cover the retina,
clouding the vision. I would see light and make out images at
the sides of the eye, but legally I was blind.

The news shattered me. You don't lose the sight of one of
your eyes casually. For months after the injury I had to visit
the hospital every week for treatments. But they weren't nearly
as painful as the ache I experienced when I thought that the
eye injury would finish me as an athlete. Sports had been such
an important part of life for me that I just couldn't stand the
thought of having to give it up.

My injury occurred in March of 1935, and naturally, it
finished my hockey playing for that season. I bided my time
until May, speculating about what would happen when I tried
to play baseball with one good eye. I wondered and I worried
and it turned out that my concerns were justified.

When I went out for the first time that spring to start
playing ball, I was crushed. I just couldn't do it. There were
all kinds of things that I had done quite naturally on a ball
field when I had two good eyes that I just couldn't do with only
one.

For example, I had been a righthanded batter all my life, but now, when I went up to the plate, I discovered I couldn't swing from that side. That's because you judge the ball with your back eye when you're swinging. So I switched to bat lefty. In the field I couldn't judge the bounce of the ball. Try closing one eye and have somebody throw you a ball or roll a ball to you. You'll find you can't catch it.

That was the worst summer of my life. I had grown up with baseball and played against future major leaguers Phil Rizzuto and Sid Gordon. Now I couldn't even judge the bounce on the easiest rollers. I was really down. If I couldn't play baseball, there was no reason to believe that I'd be able to play hockey either. I spent that whole summer wondering whether there would be some way I could still play hockey. I confess that I was plenty scared the first time I laced on a pair of skates that fall. The injury had finished me in baseball. Would it be the same in hockey? I was almost too frightened to find out.

Baseball was important to me, but hockey was always number one. I can remember throughout high school in elocution classes when you had to make a speech on what you wanted to be, I would always say I wanted to be a player in the National Hockey League. There would be snickers because everyone knew hockey was a Canadian game and there simply was very little room for Americans—especially Americans who were growing up in New York City. But that's what I wanted to be and that's why my first time on the ice after losing my eye was so important to me.

This time, I looked around as I stepped onto the ice. I skated easily around, trying to ignore the nervous feeling in my legs. I circled the rink a couple of times and then started throwing a puck around with a couple of other fellows. It didn't take me long to realize that a minor miracle had developed. The injury didn't bother my hockey a bit. I could take a pass, shoot a puck, or throw a check every bit as well after the injury as I could before it. I was thrilled. It was as if I had received a new lease on life.

I had been living on pins and needles all summer, worried about whether I'd be able to play. When I found out that I could, even with one eye, I felt higher than a kite. It was like popping the cork on a bottle of champagne and having the bubbly stuff spill all over the place. I was so grateful to be playing that I played with all of my strength, using every ounce of energy I could summon from my body. Maybe it was my trying so hard that caused me to play so well. Anyway, Tom Lockhart, general manager and coach of the New York Rovers, began noticing that wild kid who ran all over the ice for the New York Stock Exchange.

One day Lockhart came over to me in the Garden. "Hey kid," he said, "how would you like to play for the Rovers?"

He might as well have asked if I'd like a million bucks. The Rovers played in the Eastern Hockey League and served as a farm club for the New York Rangers. The EHL was a developmental league and was considered just a step away from the NHL. Did I want to play for the Rovers? It didn't take me long to answer Lockhart's question.

Lockhart's was a one-man operation, and he ran it as economically as possible. He was not very big with the buck and he kept me a Simon Pure—the equivalent of an amateur. Everybody else got paid, but I got nothing. It sure wasn't like the salaries hockey players get these days, but I didn't mind. I was so happy to be playing that I think I would have paid Lockhart if he had asked me. Come to think of it, I'm surprised he didn't.

The Rovers put me on their all-American line with Stu Iglehardt at center and Sammy Babcock on the other wing. There were some pretty good hockey players on that club—guys like Murray Armstrong, who became a collegiate coach later on, goalie Bert Gardiner, Muzz Patrick, Dunc Farmer, and others.

The Eastern League was no patsy circuit. It served as the training ground for some fine hockey players. Guys like Alex Shibicky, Neil and Mac Colville, Dutch Hiller, Cal Gardner, and lots of others all started there. It was great company for Lockhart's kid American hockey player to be keeping.

I was no great star for the Rovers—it would have been tough to outshine some of the talent Lockhart had playing for that club. They used me as a penalty killer and handyman. I was a good checker, and Lockhart would often assign me to shadow other guys around the league. One of my favorite assignments was Herb Foster of Atlantic City. Lockhart would say, "Bill, stick with that guy," and I'd become part of his uniform.

In two years with the Rovers I scored the grand total of maybe half a dozen goals. It wasn't my job to put the puck in the net, but occasionally I did. My first goal came in Baltimore against a guy named Lee. The years have dimmed the memory of that first one, and I like to think it was the climax of one of those rink-length dashes that lifts fans right out of their seats. But with me, it was probably a case of some other guy's shot hitting me in the seat of the pants and bouncing into the net.

It was quite an experience playing for the Rovers and Lockhart. I was like a moonlighter with them because I continued to play for the New York Stock Exchange team. I felt I had a moral obligation to play for the Exchange team. And there was also the matter of a weekly paycheck, which Lockhart hadn't seen fit to provide for me. He did pay $5 a day in meal money, but there was no provision for the loss of personal belongings.

When I joined the Rovers, they were in Baltimore for a game. I was so pleased with myself moving into that fast hockey company that I decided to celebrate. I went out and bought the handsomest new hat you ever did see. It was sitting jauntily on my head when Muzz Patrick, my new teammate, brought me and my hat back down to earth. Muzz grabbed the chapeau and tossed it casually under an approaching trolley car. There wasn't much of it left to retrieve when the trolley had passed, and my $5 meal money didn't exactly cover the loss, even in those depression days.

Besides Baltimore and the Rovers, the EHL was composed of Atlantic City, Pittsburgh, and Hershey. Washington and Boston were added later. It was a railroad league with the teams doing almost all of their travel on the Baltimore and Ohio. Sometimes those trips were real adventures.

Once we were playing in Pittsburgh when a flood hit. We couldn't get into the center of town, but we made it to Duquesne Garden for our game and then back to the railroad station. We were due to leave at midnight and the guys all settled back and went to sleep. When we woke up the next morning, we were still in Pittsburgh.

"What the hell is going on here?" raged Lockhart.

The railroad people tried to explain about the flood, but Tommy wasn't hearing too much of the explanation. "We have a 1:00 P.M. commitment in New York," shouted Lockhart, shaking his fist at the frightened railroad man, who probably wasn't used to dealing with an angry hockey general manager.

"What's he getting so excited about?" one of the other Rover players said, nodding at Lockhart, whose neck was beginning to turn a deep, rich red. "Our game isn't until three, not one."

I just laughed. "I'm his commitment," I said, "I've got to be at the Garden at one to play for the Stock Exchange."

Because Lockhart had a way of getting things done, the New York Rovers Hockey Club soon found itself with an engine, commandeered by the boss. We had a caboose, our car, and that engine, and off we went. When we got to Philadelphia, Lockhart ordered the Philadelphia Ramblers car attached. They were on their way to New Haven. And off we went again. Needless to say, we got to the Garden in time for Lockhart's "commitment,"—my 1:00 P.M. game.

The Rovers' trainer was Mike Hausser, who wasn't shy when it came to indulging in a little pregame cheer, liquid or otherwise. Hausser used to rub my legs between my double-header each Sunday. I'd come off the ice after playing for the Stock Exchange, get my rubdown from Hausser, and then go right back out and play for the Rovers.

One time, Hausser was feeling no pain and started splashing his liniment all over me with no concern for where the hot stuff went. Lockhart loved the idea because some of Hausser's liniment landed in the wrong place, and I really flew in that second game.

I was with the Rovers during the 1935–1936 and 1936–1937 seasons and enjoyed moderate success, especially when you consider that I was playing with only one eye. I doubled up with the Stock Exchange team throughout that time and hockey was taking up a substantial part of my life, a situation I thoroughly enjoyed. I was so involved in my hockey playing activities that there were times I completely forgot my handicap. It seemed to be as natural for me to get along with one eye as other people functioned with full vision in both eyes. I never even thought about it until one day late in the 1937 season.

I was playing for the Rovers and skated into a corner for the puck. You know the kind of scrambles you get when a couple of players pile up together. Well, anyway, I was in there with my face. I got hit at the corner of my left eye—my good eye—and the blade cut me. In the space of a few seconds, blood was spilling into my eye and for a terrifying moment, I couldn't see a thing.

I thought to myself, "Oh, no, my good eye. I'm blind." My whole life flashed through my mind as I fell to the ice, blood gushing from the wound.

Somebody up there must have been watching over me at

that moment. After the doctor had wiped the blood from my eye and stitched the cut, he patted me on the shoulder. "Okay, young man," he said, "I'm done. You're finished in here."

I got up from the doctor's table and realized that he wasn't the only one who was finished. It had been just too close a call for me. That horrible sinking feeling I had at the moment when I thought that stick had hit my good eye was just too much to take. I realized then and there that I was done, too—done with playing hockey. The risk was just too great. Nobody loved this game more than I did, but I realized that this was a losing proposition for me. I had lost one eye and I just couldn't take the chance of losing the other as well. As much as it hurt—and it hurt plenty—I was ready to walk away from the game.

That was a sad time for me, but I had no choice. My hockey playing days were over. And so, it seemed, was my dream of being an American in the NHL. But just because I couldn't play hockey, that didn't mean I couldn't watch the game. While my left eye healed, I still showed up at Madison Square Garden each Sunday to watch the Rovers play. I became just another spectator, watching the world's best spectator sport. I can't say I enjoyed that seat in the stands because, frankly, I ached to be out there on the ice.

In March 1937 I showed up as usual for an EHL game involving the Rovers at the Garden. I was sitting upstairs, watching the teams warm up when the announcement came over the public address system: "Bill Chadwick, please report to the penalty timekeeper's bench.

I made my way down through the stands, and when I got to rinkside, there was Tommy Lockhart, waiting for me. "Bill, we're in trouble," he said. "Ray Levia is stuck in a snowstorm and he can't make it."

I knew Levia. He had played in the Eastern League with the Atlantic City Seagulls before retiring to become a referee in the league. What did he have to do with me, I wondered?

"Bill," said Lockhart, hesitating the way he did when he was getting ready to ask you for a favor, "would you try to referee this game?"

I looked at Tommy rather incredulously. Was he serious?

"Bill, I need a referee and I'd appreciate it if you'd try it," said Lockhart.

That was all I had to hear. It was the game of hockey, and if it meant trying to stand on my head, I would do it, because it's the greatest game in the world.

I looked at Lockhart and nodded. "Where's the whistle?" I asked.

Tommy grinned. "Thanks, Bill," he said.

My skates were still in the Rovers dressing room at the Garden, and I quickly laced them on. I was wearing the damnedest referee outfit you'll ever see. I had on a pair of brown and white checked pants and Lockhart found a sweatshirt for me. He handed me the whistle, and away I went.

The first period was quiet enough and I got through it all right. During the intermission I was sitting in the dressing room, my head swimming from the situation I suddenly was in. Into the room walked Lockhart, who not only ran the Rovers but also doubled as boss of the EHL. I looked up, expecting him to tell me that Levia had shown up and that I could go back to my seat. It never happened.

"Bill," said Lockhart, "you're doing fine. But why do you keep your hands in your pockets?"

I laughed at the question. "I keep them there because I don't know what the hell else to do with them," I told Tommy.

"Well, do something with them," said Lockhart, "but get 'em out of your pockets."

"Okay," I said. "Watch me this next period and let me know what you think after that."

In that second period I found out what to do with my hands. I waved them all over the place. When I called a penalty, I pointed at the offending player and I shouted. "Number 5, I want you for two minutes, tripping!" Then I'd bring my hand back across my leg in a tripping motion.

The players gave me an odd sort of look when I started using signals. It had never been done in hockey before. But it helped me get rid of some of my nervous energy and I felt more relaxed when I did it. It also made me feel like I really had control of the game. After all, that's the most important thing for an official in any sport.

After the second period Lockhart was back again. "That's better, Bill. Keep it up."

I took the advice and kept it up for the next 18 years. And because I had learned my lesson the hard way, I always kept my eye on the puck.

3

THE TELEGRAM

After I refereed that first Eastern League game, Tommy Lockhart collared me in the dressing room. I was unlacing my skates when he came through the door. I peered up at him and he had a big grin on his face. Lockhart's grin could light up a whole room, so I smiled back at him.

"What are you so happy about?" I asked.

"You," he said. "You did great out there. How would you like to continue refereeing?"

I shrugged. I hadn't really ever thought about officiating hockey games. I was always too busy playing them. But with one eye gone and recalling that sinking feeling when I stopped a hockey stick with the other one, I knew I was through playing this game. Maybe I could referee it. Hockey was all I ever wanted to do with my life from the time I was a kid, and certainly that would be one way to stay in the game. Maybe Lockhart had something there.

"Tom, do you really think I could?" I asked him.

"Sure!" he said, patting me on the back. "You were great today and you'll be great all the time."

Now Lockhart was no fool. He knew he couldn't break me right into the Eastern League. I had handled that one game all right, but I'd need experience elsewhere before I could be ready for that league full-time. And Lockhart had just the place for me to get the experience.

"Well start you in the Metropolitan League," he said. "You'll referee those games and you can line the Eastern League games."

So, there I was, doing Madison Square Garden double-headers again every Sunday, only now I was an official instead of a player. And those two games were really the easiest parts of my weekends. I knew I needed experience, so I went looking for hockey games to referee. I found some in my old haunting grounds, the Brooklyn Ice Palace.

The Catholic High School League used to run triple-headers at the Ice Palace every Saturday morning. I refereed all three games and was rewarded with $5 for my services. But I gained a lot more than that in experience. Then I also did "dark-house" games—no fans in the building, just players and me. So by the time I got around to doing the Met League games, I had plenty of warmup action.

In those days Pat Kennedy was probably the best-known sports official around. He was a basketball referee, and he went through all sorts of contortions on the court when he called a foul or a jump ball. On the ice I was becoming hockey's Pat Kennedy. I gestured at the players and gradually developed my own particular set of hand signals. After all, I had to keep my hands out of my pockets to make Lockhart happy.

When I called a penalty, I waved my hands and went into a lot of motions. At first it helped hide my own nervousness, but eventually the penalty signals developed. I grabbed my wrist for holding, rolled my arms for charging, slapped my hand across my leg for tripping, and raised my hands together for a high stick. Soon I was putting on a pretty good show. I guess Lockhart must have thought so too, because the next year he gave me a job as an Eastern League referee.

My salary was to be $55 per week, which wasn't bad until you consider that the $55 also was supposed to cover all my expenses. There were two divisions and two referees. While one ref worked the southern leg of the league in Washington and Baltimore, the other one made the northern circuit of Atlantic City, New York, and River Vale, New Jersey. A week on the road paying for meals, room and board, and travel took a good chunk out of that $55 and I was just about in the same position financially as I had been when I was making $15 a week clear profit playing for the New York Stock Exchange. I was a referee instead of a player, but working for Lockhart, I was still virtually a Simon Pure.

A typical week for an EHL ref might start on a Tuesday in Baltimore. The next night the scene was Washington. Then back to Baltimore on Thursday and a return to Washington on Friday. Whenever I went to the southern sector, I traveled by train. When I worked the northern route, I borrowed dad's car to get around and then saved a little of Lockhart's $55.

Pop encouraged my refereeing with as much enthusiasm as he had given me when I was playing hockey. You were always alone in the Eastern League. The home team provided the linesman and minor officials. Sometimes, the puck would be at center ice and the goal light would go on. In the visiting team's end there often seemed to be lead in the goal judge's finger, but in the home team's end there was lightning in the judge's fingers. The only unbiased official in the building was me, and sometimes it got a little lonely out there. Then I'd look over at the penalty box and see dad rooting for me. It was the greatest feeling, and it got me over a lot of rough spots.

One of those rough spots happened in Washington, D.C., and in all the years I was connected with hockey it was the only time I've ever seen anything suggesting an attempt to fix a game. I was in the referee's dressing room before a game when the icemaker came in. He had a wad of bills rolled up in his hand.

"Hi, Chadwick," he said. "Listen, I've got a bundle bet on this game and. . . ."

He never finished the sentence because I showed him to the door, not taking any particular care over my manners or lack of them with the bum. The next day I called Tom Lockhart and told him what had happened. The next time I refereed a game in Washington, there was a different icemaker in the building.

Often, amateur teams from Canada would come to the United States to play exhibition games against Eastern League clubs. I was assigned to referee some of those games against teams like the Port Colborne Sailors and Toronto Goodyears, and it must have been a new experience for those touring teams to get a fair shake from an official. Anyway, I can remember that one of the Toronto club officials came to me after a game and thanked me for calling a fair game. His name was Powers, and his son, Eddie Powers, later refereed in the National Hockey League. Powers and other team officials took a liking to me, and when they went home, they took with them word of a young kid from New York who gave visiting teams a square deal when he refereed. Eventually, that word reached the NHL and its president, Frank Calder.

Calder had served as president of the NHL from its inception in 1917, and anybody who could survive that long surrounded by the egotists who ran the member clubs had to be a great man. Anyway, Calder began asking around about this young American referee, Bill Chadwick. Two of the people he asked were Lester Patrick, general manager of the New York Rangers, and Red Dutton, who had the same job with the New York Americans.

The Rangers and Americans both played in Madison Square Garden, but they were like the prince and the pauper. The Rangers were owned by the Garden management and the Americans were just tenants. Dutton never really appreciated that second-class kind of status, and his objections to it turned out to be very important for me.

The NHL was very much like the EHL in that all games had two officials—a referee appointed by the league and a linesman, provided by the home team. Madison Square Garden's house linesman was Fred Stevenson, and he worked both the Rangers and Americans games. Dutton didn't like that idea—sharing the Rangers linesman. He wanted one of his own and he told Calder so. Red also had a candidate in mind.

"How about that kid Chadwick?" he asked Calder. "He's a good referee. He could do the job."

"I don't know," said Calder. "Let me think about it for a while."

Of course, while all of this was going on, I didn't know anything about it. I just went about my business of refereeing the EHL games the best way I knew how. Sometimes it wasn't easy. The league was no bed of roses, and I had my share of problems. The worst one happened in 1939, my second year in the EHL.

I was assigned to officiate in a game in River Vale, New Jersey, between the New York Rovers and the River Vale Skeeters. Their rivalry was the hottest in the Eastern League because the Rovers served as a farm club for the New York Rangers and River Vale was the farm club of the New York Americans. The Rangers and Amerks weren't the best of friends and their dislike for one another carried right over to the Rovers and Skeeters. No game between those two clubs would ever be easy, and when the games were played in River Vale, things got even worse.

John Handwerg, who was a successful golf course builder, owned the River Vale Arena and he was concerned with keeping his crowds happy, so he installed a bar running the whole length of one side of the rink. And he'd run around like crazy, all charged up, ranting and raving. Unless every whistle that was blown was in his team's favor, there was a little ruckus. I had a habit of not blowing every whistle in his favor.

Early in the first period I called one of River Vale's

players for holding. I gave it the full treatment, pointing at the offending player and shouting, "I want you! Two minutes for holding," while gripping my wrist to signal the penalty. Handwerg didn't agree with the call.

"You showboat, Chadwick, get in the game, will you?" he yelled.

I ignored him, figuring he'd calm down later on. It never happened. He was on me every time I blew the whistle. If I made a call in River Vale's favor, he'd holler something sarcastic like, "It's about time you opened your eyes." If I called one against River Vale, his comments were really nasty.

By the time the third period rolled around, Handwerg had worked me over pretty thoroughly. He had given me absolutely the worst time I'd ever had with anybody in connection with this game. And in that third period a terrible thing happened. The constant harangue, the needling, the cussing—all of it just piled too high for me to handle.

As I skated up and down the ice trying to follow the action and trying to block out the tongue-lashing I was taking, I could feel the pressure building up inside of me. I fought to control my emotions, but I could feel tears welling in my eyes. My brain was splitting. Every time another heckler jumped on the bandwagon his words cut right through me and etched themselves in my brain.

"Showboat!"

"Stiff!"

"Bum!"

I'll never know how I ever made it through that last period in River Vale, but somehow I did. When I got to the dressing room, all of the emotion that had built up inside of me spilled over. I sat on the bench, my head in my hands, and I cried like a baby.

"I'm through," I sobbed. "I can't take this anymore. I'm finished with hockey. I'll never referee another game."

I was shaking. The bottom of my world had just about

fallen out. Then I felt a hand on my shoulder. I looked up, and there was Tommy Lockhart.

"Bill, what's wrong?" he asked.

"Tom, I just can't take it anymore. The pressure's too much for me. I'm no good at this refereeing business. I'm finished with hockey."

Lockhart sat down next to me on the dressing room bench, smiling his soft Irish smile. He's a very compassionate man—hard-hearted on the outside but with a soft spot in him, too. And this young referee needed some compassion at that moment.

"Now, now, Bill," he said. "Let's not be so hasty. I want you to go home for a week and think things out. Don't rush into anything, and promise me you'll talk to me before you decide anything."

"Tommy, it won't do any good," I protested. "I've had it. I'm just no good at this thing."

But Lockhart wouldn't give up. He knew I was only 24 years old and he knew how much I loved hockey. And he wasn't ready to let me lock myself out of the game.

I was still convinced Lockhart was barking up the wrong tree, but I agreed to do what he suggested. The next week I was scheduled to move into the Eastern League's southern tier—Washington and Baltimore—to relieve Frank McGaffin, the league's other referee. It was McGaffin's turn to come home and do the northern zone. But when Lockhart gave me that week off, McGaffin got stuck in the southern sector for an extra week. I don't think Frank, who is now an official scorer for the New York Rangers, has ever quite forgiven me for that extra week he had to spend in Washington and Baltimore.

During that week at home I did a lot of thinking, and I must admit that hockey was losing. After all, I could still go back to work for the New York Stock Exchange and probably carve out a fair career for myself there. The abuse I had taken was just not worth it. Why should I subject myself to that sort of thing? That was the way I felt until the moment the doorbell rang and the telegram was delivered.

Telegrams always carry with them a sense of urgency, especially when you're not expecting them. And I wasn't expecting this one. It was from Montreal, headquarters of the National Hockey League. It was simple and to the point. It said I was to report to Madison Square Garden on such and such a date to serve as a linesman for the New York Americans.

My whole outlook changed. It was as if I was walking down the street and some stranger stepped up to me and handed me a crisp new $1,000 bill. To be appointed a linesman in the NHL was just the ultimate happening. And what compounded the situation was my being an American citizen, a fact that couldn't have worked in my favor when my name came up for consideration. There weren't many Americans playing hockey in the NHL, and there were even fewer officials. I called Tom Lockhart immediately.

"That's great news, Bill," said Lockhart when I read him Calder's telegram. "Are you going to take it?"

I laughed.

My resignation from Tommy Lockhart's Eastern League was premature. "Bill, just because you're lining in the National Hockey League is no reason to stop refereeing in our league," argued Lockhart. "The experience will be good for you, and I'll still keep you on full salary."

The first part of Lockhart's plea sounded good, but not the second. Working in the old Eastern League was like being in the army—you'd never get rich. But Tommy was right about the experience I could get in the EHL. I guess he could tell I was thinking about staying, and once Lockhart has a hunch that you're even casually considering one of his ideas, he swarms in on you to put it over. He's a persuasive Irishman and he persuaded me.

"Okay," I said. "I'll stay and do both."

4

MY FIRST STANLEY CUP

My appointment as an NHL linesman came late in the 1939 hockey season, and I will never forget the first game I worked at Madison Square Garden. The Montreal Canadiens were in town to play the Americans, and all that day I was jumpy and jittery, anticipating my first assignment. When it was finally time to leave for the Garden, I just about flew out of the house.

I got down early to the old Garden on Eighth Avenue between Forty-ninth and Fiftieth streets. As I crossed the street, I looked up at the canopy-type marquee that hung over the awesome building, fully expecting it to read: "TONIGHT'S LINESMAN—BILL CHADWICK." The Garden chose instead to advertise the appearance of the Canadiens.

That was all right, though. I knew I was going to be there, and that was enough. I bounced along Forty-ninth Street with a lilt in my step and went through the employee entrance down the long corridor that led to the officials' dressing room. I was not only the first official in the building but virtually the only person in the whole building. I tossed my equipment bag in a corner and began to dress for my first assignment in the NHL.

My hands were cold as I fumbled with my skates, feeling

every bit as nervous as any rookie has ever felt in any sport. I was tying my skates, or at least trying to, when I heard a noise at the door. I looked up to see Bill Stewart walk in. He was that night's referee.

I got up and walked over. "Hi, Mr. Stewart," I said, extending my hand. "I'm your linesman, Bill Chadwick."

Stewart smiled. "Hi, kid," he said, shaking hands. "Your first game?"

I nodded, feeling that damn clammy cold sensation surging through my body again.

"Don't worry about it," said Stewart. "You'll be okay."

I forced a smile and Stewart grinned back. Slowly, he began to climb out of his street clothes and dress for the game. I watched him with the kind of awe young hockey players reserve today for players like Bobby Hull and Bobby Orr.

Stewart wasn't a big man. He was built close to the ground, stumpy in a way, something like a fireplug. He spent his summers as an umpire in baseball's National League and is the only official I know who worked in two major leagues at the same time. He was a proud man and it showed when he hit the ice.

He'd skate around like the cock of the walk, his chest all swelled up. He was prancing around, making sure everybody in the building knew who he was. And everybody did, not only because of his refereeing and umpiring background but because he had coached the Chicago Black Hawks to a Stanley Cup the year before when the Chicago Black Hawks seemed about as likely to win the Cup as the New York Islanders are today.

The owner of the Black Hawks was Major Fred Mc-Laughlin, whose operation of the team might be charitably described as erratic. The major had ten coaches in six seasons, one of them a friendly fan who had met the owner on a train and offered some suggestions. In 1937 he hired Stewart as general manager and coach.

Now Stewart didn't exactly have a powerhouse team. In fact, his club was one of the weakest in the league, winning only 14 of 48 regular-season games. But that was good enough for third place in the NHL's American Division and a spot in the playoffs. And when they started playing for the Stanley Cup, Stewart's team turned into world-beaters.

In each of the first two rounds they lost the opening game and then came back to eliminate first the Montreal Canadiens and then the New York Americans. That put the Black Hawks in the finals against the Toronto Maple Leafs, champions of the Canadian Division and losers of only 15 of their 48 regular-season games. Clearly, Stewart's team was in over its head.

As if the spectre of playing Toronto wasn't bad enough, Stewart had an added headache. His ace goalie, Mike Karakas, came up with an injured toe before the first game and had to be scratched from the lineup. I admired Karakas because like me, he was an American, born in Aurora, Minnesota, and a star in the Canadian game of hockey.

Stewart appealed to the Maple Leafs to let him use the Rangers' goalie, Davey Kerr, as a replacement for Karakas. But Conn Smythe, boss of the Toronto club, was having none of that, and the Black Hawks wound up with a minor leaguer, Alfie Moore, in goal. Stewart's "discussion" with Smythe over his goalie before the game was spiced by a brief jostling match between the two men. I could understand that, knowing them both.

When Moore beat the Maple Leafs in the opener, he skated off the ice, thumbing his nose at the Toronto bench. Frank Calder the league president, ruled him ineligible for the second game, and the Hawks came up with another minor league goalie, Paul Goodman, who was fished out of a movie theater just two hours before the game began. This time Toronto won, 5–1, tying the series.

For game three, Karakas recovered and the Black Hawks won, 2–1, on a goal scored by Doc Romnes with 4:05 left in the game. The Leafs argued that the puck had hit the post and bounced back out, but they were overruled by the referee, a Rhodes scholar named Clarence Campbell. That was the turning point. Chicago won the next game, and the Stanley Cup, in the best three-out-of-five series.

In the dressing room Major McLaughlin hugged Stewart and acclaimed his coach a genius. All I can say is that Bill must have gotten stupid very fast, because in the middle of the next season McLaughlin fired him.

His dismissal as Chicago coach didn't faze Stewart a bit. He just returned to his old job as an NHL referee, and if he called games involving the Black Hawks just a little bit closer than others, well, you could understand why.

So that's how Bill Stewart, who had been drinking champagne out of the Stanley Cup the season before, and Bill Chadwick, who had been calling penalties in River Vale, New Jersey, the week before, happened to be in the same dressing room at Madison Square Garden, preparing to officiate a National Hockey League game.

As we skated to center ice for the playing of the National Anthem, Stewart and I lined up along with the starting teams for the Canadiens and Americans. An enormous swelling of pride surged through me as I stood stiffly at attention through the final bars of "The Star-Spangled Banner." I had made it. The New York-born Yank was in the NHL.

Stewart dropped the puck at center ice and the game was underway. Almost from that moment the Canadiens' bench was on Stewart. They called him every name in the book and a couple that probably weren't in the book.

"You couldn't coach and you can't ref," one of them yelled.

"Go back to baseball, you bum," hollered another. "You need glasses, Stewart."

Every so often, I'd steal a glance at Stewart and I could see his neck getting progressively redder as the Canadiens kept riding him. Of course, Red Dutton and the Americans weren't exactly the picture of decorum either, and they were also raising hell with Stewart. Things got so bad for a while that I thought I was back in River Vale, New Jersey, with John Handwerg hollering at me. But this time I wasn't the target. Stewart was and the proud little peacock didn't like it one bit.

After the second period—a particularly rough one for Stewart—we were toweling off in the dressing room when Stewart strolled over to me. I looked up at him, not knowing what to expect. The last thing I expected was what he said next.

"Kid," said Stewart. "Don't leave me now. Stay right with me. After this game, we are going into the Montreal Canadiens' dressing room."

Now wouldn't that make a dandy picture? A referee and linesman going into a hockey team's dressing room for a little discussion with the coach and a dozen or so players. Just dandy.

I didn't know what to do when Stewart laid that line on me. I thought he had to be nuts, but I felt I ought to go along with the referee. It was my job to help him as much as I could, but I must admit that I wondered if that responsibility included trips into a team's dressing room. But I was new at this and so wrapped up in the game that I didn't even really know what Stewart wanted in the Canadiens' room.

I should have guessed. The Garden police did. Fortunately for Stewart and me, they blocked our way to the dressing room and kept us out. It's a good thing they did. If they hadn't, this story might be ending right here.

When I broke in as a linesman, there were three regular referees in the NHL. Stewart was one, and the other two were Frank "King" Clancy and Mickey Ion. Clancy was a former defenseman who weighed maybe 150 pounds if you got him on the scale after dinner, but he had more guts than a steeplejack. Ion was a former lacrosse player who refereed games with such total detachment that Clancy once said, "There's nothing but ice water running through his veins."

I worked with all three of them through the remainder of the 1939 season and all of 1940 when I was rehired as an NHL linesman. I guess I must have been doing a good job, or at least Ion thought so.

"There are going to be some changes made in this league," he kept telling me. "They're going to make you a referee and they're going to do it next year." I kept laughing him off, but down deep I hoped the old ref knew what he was talking about.

All through the 1940 hockey season I lined in the NHL, refereed in Tommy Lockhart's Eastern League, and continued to work at the New York Stock Exchange. It was a hectic schedule, but somehow I kept up with it. The Exchange was particularly good to me, letting me take time off when I had to because of my hockey duties. I didn't get paid for the time, but at least I had a home and a job to come back to when there were no more hockey games to officiate.

At the end of the 1940 season I got word from the NHL office in Montreal that I was to serve as a linesman for the playoffs. My first assignment was to be in Boston for a game between the Bruins and the Toronto Maple Leafs. It was an NHL tradition then, and still is now, to import minor officials like goal judges and penalty timekeepers from noncompeting cities for the playoffs to insure impartiality. For the Boston series, the New York minor officials were assigned.

One of the New York officials was a fellow named Dick Williams. He had a big Cadillac and was driving the others up to Boston. I hitched a ride with them and we left the city in plenty of time for a nice, leisurely drive north. It was almost too leisurely.

Williams' car started huffing and puffing when we got to Connecticut. We stalled out a half-dozen times, and every

time the car conked out, I'd glance at my watch and start wor-
rying about that eight o'clock face-off in Boston Garden. By
the time we got to New Haven, Williams' car gave one last
horrible gasp and died. Here we were, 175 miles from Boston
and my first playoff assignment. I just kept thinking about
Mickey Ion dressing to referee the game and looking for his
linesman.

We rushed to the train station and grabbed the first railroad man we could find. "When's the next train to Boston?" I
demanded, an urgency in my voice that seemed to shake the
railroad man.

"It will be along in a while," he said casually, indifferent
to the urgency of our situation.

It seemed forever before the New Haven Railroad's next
Boston-bound train found its way into the New Haven station.
We all jumped on and again I glanced at my watch. The news
wasn't good. We had one thing going for us, though. The
train would pull into South Station in Boston, a quick cab ride
from the Boston Garden, where the Bruins played. Too bad
the train didn't arrive at North Station, because the Garden is
built right over the railroad terminal.

I remember rushing out of the train when it finally
reached Boston after what seemed an eternity of whistle-stop-
ping its way through northern Connecticut and southern
Massachusetts. I grabbed the first cab I saw and it shot over to
the Garden. I looked at the big clock in the lobby and it said
7:55.

"Five minutes to face-off," I thought to myself.

I literally ran into the building and down the tunnel
under the stands to the referee's dressing room. Outside the
room stood a man, his arms folded, one eye on his wristwatch
and the other on that tunnel. Frank Calder, president of the
National Hockey League, was waiting for Bill Chadwick,
rookie linesman.

Calder was looking at me sternly, and I knew he was wondering what kind of official I could be if I couldn't even get to the game on time.

"Good evening, Mr. Calder," I said brightly, trying to hide the quiver in my voice. "We had some car trouble. I'll be ready in a minute."

Now I know that Ion couldn't have cared less if I showed up a minute before the game started or a minute after it ended. He could have handled it all by himself and never batted an eye. He was that kind of guy. But that wasn't the idea. Here I was, just getting my feet wet in the league and handed my first playoff assignment, and I had almost blown it. I was an inexperienced kid and I hadn't taken the proper precautions. It wasn't the broken-down old Cadillac's fault. It was mine. If Calder had given me a good swift kick in the pants, I would have understood. I deserved one.

But Calder never said a word. He just stood there, arms folded, face frozen. I smiled again and rushed past him into the dressing room to get ready for the game. And when Ion dropped the puck at center ice to start the action, I was at his side, ready to go.

Frank Brimsek shut out the Maple Leafs that night, winning, 3-0, and the next day I was scheduled to head for Montreal, where I was going to line the second game of the Canadiens' series against Chicago. Now you'd think with all of the travel headaches I'd had getting to Boston that the law of averages would be on my side for this trip—by train. I was due for a soft one, wasn't I? Maybe so, but I didn't get one. For the second straight trip, I ran into all sorts of difficulties and again I was nearly late for an assignment.

But this time, I had an ace in the hole. One of the other passengers on our delayed Montreal train ride happened to be dear old Frank Calder, my boss. It was like riding in the pocket of the Lord.

The referee for the game was my friend, King Clancy.

When you went out to line a game in which Clancy was the referee, you never knew what was going to happen. He'd drop the puck and say, "All right, you bastards, any way you want to play, you play, and any way I want to call it, I'll call it." Most of the time he'd skate up and down the ice and yell, "Look out for the trip," or "Look out for the hold." But he'd call very few of them. Yet he was still an efficient official and a good referee. The reason for that was that he refereed games with common sense, the most important quality any official in any sport can possess.

They give you a rule book and it hasn't changed a whole hell of a lot in the 30 years I've been associated with the game. It wasn't worth a damn then and it isn't worth a damn now. If you don't referee a game with common sense, you might as well throw that damn whistle away, because it isn't worth anything to you.

If you refereed strictly by the book without interpreting those rules and using your head for something besides a hat rack, you'd have nobody on the ice and fewer people in the building. Clancy had the ability to referee with that basic quality of common sense, and that's what made him such a good one.

Clancy was the referee and I was the linesman on April 12, 1941, when Boston defeated Detroit, 3-1, to clinch the Stanley Cup. It was the last game I ever lined and it was also my last appearance in the NHL as a bachelor.

For three years I had been dating Millie Jordan, the prettiest young girl you could imagine. Millie and I had gone to Jamaica High together although she was a few years behind me. We knew each other there but never dated. Then, a few years later, we bumped into each other on the subway station on the way to work. We both got on at the same station and rode the train together. I guess you could call it a subway romance. Two weeks after the end of the 1941 hockey season we got married.

Millie didn't know the first thing about hockey when she met me. She learned fast, though, because I had a beautiful shiner when we started going together. That was a result of my second serious eye injury, another hockey souvenir. My eye looked like a rainbow thanks to that errant stick. I guess that just one look at that shiner helped Millie understand from the start that I had two love affairs going—one with her and the other with hockey.

I'm playing for the Floral Park Maroons at Madison Square Garden.

My Jamaica High team: I'm the guy with the cap in the middle. The year is 1932.

My first job as a referee was in the
Eastern League.

Millie and me on our first anniversary in
Daytona Beach, Florida, 1942

I blow the Big Whistle in the big league, the NHL. (*UPI*)

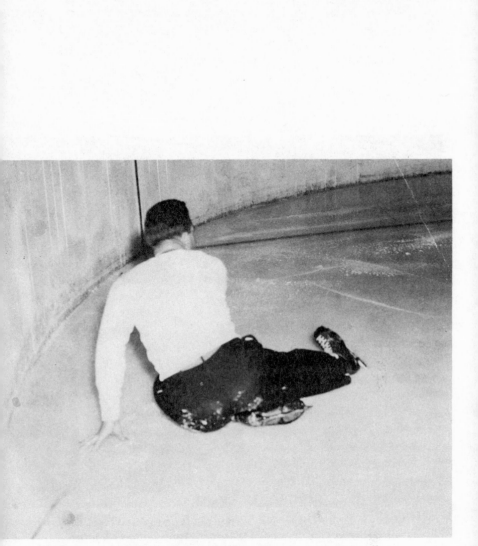

I wasn't always on my two feet. I hit the ice here in Toronto.

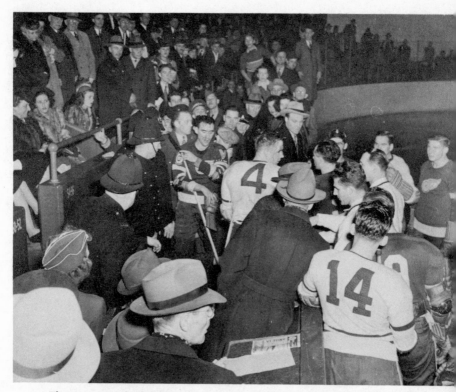

That's me on the lower right, sorting out the penalties after this blood bath between Toronto's Bob Davidson (4) and Detroit's Murray Armstrong (next to the policeman).

My best friend in hockey, King Clancy, joins me at the Boston Garden to watch, of all things, an afternoon basketball game. We had a hockey game there that night.

All in a night's work: While I'm debating with Toronto's Tom O'Neill, there's another discussion involving Montreal's Toe Blake (right), Murph Chamberlain, and the minor officials.

I like to say that I was always on top of the play—sometimes the player. This all happened in 1951 in Madison Square Garden when Detroit's Marty Pavelich scored against the Rangers. (*UPI*)

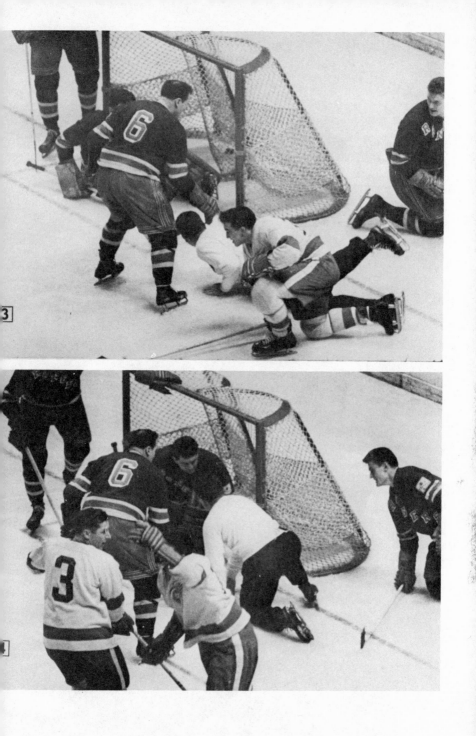

That's two minutes for hooking. Montreal's Murph Chamberlain gets the word from the Big Whistle. (*Hockey Hall of Fame*)

King Clancy has the floor, George Gravel is on the left, and I'm in the middle next to George Hayes at an NHL meeting in 1947. (*UPI*)

Maurice "Rocket" Richard, eyes aglow. I always respected him as a player but not as a man. (*Scotty Kilpatrick*)

Bill Barilko has just won the 1951 Stanley Cup for Toronto over Montreal. That's me at the side of the net as the puck flies in. It was the last goal Barilko ever scored. Before the next season began, he was lost in a plane crash. (*Wide World*)

After I retired in 1955, Clarence Campbell, president of the NHL, presented me with a silver platter acknowledging my 16 years in the league. (*Wide World*)

When I became manager of the Pine Hollow Country Club on Long Island, New York, Clarence Campbell (8-handicap, I think) came to play.

This is the sketch of me that hangs in the Hockey Hall of Fame in Toronto. (*Hockey Hall of Fame*)

Reunion of Hall of Fame referees: Frank Udvari (left) and Cooper Smeaton flank me on the night in 1968 when they closed the Fiftieth Street Madison Square Garden.

I'm accepting the Al Laney Award given by the writers "for service to New York hockey." For a change, broadcaster Marv Albert listens to my play-by-play. (*Les Rosner*)

Bobby Orr is like a gear-shift car: He can change speeds whenever he wants to, and that's an awesome weapon. (*Robert B. Shaver*)

This was the middle of that April night in 1973 when I used a bullhorn at LaGuardia Airport to plead for restraint by Ranger fans. They were wildly welcoming home the team after it had ousted the Boston Bruins in the Stanley Cup playoffs. (*Paul Bereswill*)

Some people think I'm outspoken, but I can't help that. There's no changing Bill Chadwick at this stage of the game. (*Les Rosner*)

My broadcast partner, Jim Gordon, laughs at one of my old jokes, and so do I. (*Les Rosner*)

5
OUT OF THE WAR

All through the 1940-1941 hockey season I kept hearing from Mickey Ion and other people who ought to know that I'd be refereeing in the NHL the following season. When you hear that kind of talk often enough and want it to be true as much as I did, you begin to believe it. And once I became convinced that Ion's prediction was more than idle talk, Millie and I got married. We did it on the strength of my going from $22 a week as a stock exchange page boy and $5.50 per game as an Eastern League referee to $5,000 a year in the NHL.

We got married in April, and in September the word came officially from the NHL. Bill Stewart was leaving the league and his replacement would be the kid from New York.

I guess you could call me the game's token American. Stewart was from Boston and his departure left the league without a United States citizen on the refereeing staff for a game that had seven big league teams, five of them in the United States. So, you see, instead of hurting me in hockey, my United States citizenship probably helped.

It was ironic that I replaced Bill Stewart since Stewart had been the ref for the first game I ever lined in the NHL. And what was even more ironic was that Ion, who kept predicting changes for the 1941 season, turned out to be involved in one of the changes himself. He was also removed from the refereeing staff and named referee-in-chief. His replacement was Norman Lamport, whose brother was mayor of Toronto. The other referee was King Clancy, and he was the only hold-over on the staff. That was it. Three referees—Clancy, Chadwick, and Lamport.

My official notification of appointment came in a letter from Frank Calder on September 24, 1941. I was 26 years old, and a little more than four years had elapsed since Tommy Lockhart handed me that whistle at the Eastern League game in Madison Square Garden and told me to take my hands out of my pockets.

When the news hit the floor of the stock exchange, it created a great deal of excitement. Most of the brokers and other pages knew of my involvement with hockey, and when they heard I had been picked to referee in the game's major league, well, they were almost as elated as I was.

I would be one of the youngest officials ever in the NHL, and many of the players I'd be ordering around would be older than I was. But that didn't bother me a bit. I figured I could command respect and keep order simply by skating as fast as any man on the ice and staying on top of the play. There hadn't been many complaints about the way I lined NHL games, and I didn't expect any more now that I was a referee. But that was a pipe dream that ended with the very first game I refereed in the NHL.

Calder didn't give me a softie for my starting assignment. My debut was scheduled for Madison Square Garden, and the opponents were to be the New York Rangers and the New York Americans.

Because the Americans had to pay rent to the Garden and the Rangers did not, the Americans always seemed to have financial problems. During the depression days when all America was suffering, the hockey Americans would sink in a sea of red ink. The situation became so desperate that it seemed the only thing that could bail the club out was a millionaire. Fortunately for the Amerks, the father of defenseman Red Dutton happened to be a millionaire.

The Dutton Contracting Business began diverting funds to the Americans to keep them afloat, so it's not exactly surprising that the family defenseman eventually became coach and general manager of the hockey club. By 1941 even the contracting funds were running out, so the league took over operation of the Amerks, retaining Dutton as boss and general soothsayer for the club.

So there was Dutton on one side of the ice and Lester Patrick as general manager and Frank Boucher as coach of the Rangers on the other side. And there was Chadwick, making his refereeing debut, right in the middle.

As I headed for the Garden for that opening game, I thought about how I'd handle myself. I had to assert myself, and I had to do it fast or those guys would run me right out of the building. I had seen some of the intimidation of officials that went on in the NHL and I was determined that it wasn't going to happen to me. I was proud of being a referee and I was determined to do the best damn job I could.

I decided that the answer was to stay off the boards and follow the flow of the play. You can't see the play from the boards. I also decided that when I made a call, everybody in the building would know it. I'd shout, "You tripped him!" or "You slashed him!" just the way I had in the Eastern League. And I'd use those hand signals that kept my hands out of my pockets. Okay, I said to myself. I'm ready for anything they try.

I dressed quickly, trying not to let myself think about the game. I knew if I did, my nervousness would surface. Nevertheless, as I finished tying my skates, I got that clammy, cold feeling one experiences in times of stress. Then I thought back to all those dim, dark rinks with the chicken wire fencing instead of glass and the Brooklyn Ice Palace with its weird hockey dimensions and extra poles sticking up out of the ice in the defensive zones. If I had survived all those places and if I had survived the loss of my right eye and the near loss of my left one, well, I could damn well survive the Rangers and the Americans and Dutton and Patrick.

"Let's go," I said, adjusting the referee's sweater with the NHL crest over the heart.

The game started serenely enough and for the first six or seven minutes nothing very controversial happened. Then there was a whistle for an icing violation, and across the ice came Tommy Anderson, captain of the Americans, headed for me. *What the hell does he want?* I wondered. I soon found out.

"Hey, rook," said Anderson. "Dutton wants to see you."

I looked over at the Americans' bench and there was Dutton waving at me to come over for a little conversation. He knew I was a busher, and I could see by the look in his eye that he was going to give me some unsolicited instructions. It was a regular method of intimidation for coaches to do that and it worked very often. I made up my mind that it wasn't going to work on me.

"Well," I told Anderson, "you go back to Dutton and tell him I don't want to see him. And you can also tell him that if we don't start playing, he's going to get a two-minute penalty for delay of the game.

As soon as I told Anderson off, I felt great. The nervousness virtually disappeared. I had shown Dutton that I wasn't his linesman anymore. I was an NHL referee now and I wasn't going to be intimidated by him or any other coach or manager in this league. Somehow I knew I had just done something that would be very important for my reputation.

Anderson skated over to Dutton and delivered my message. Red's face lit up, and there was rage in his eyes. How could Chadwick do that? No referee ever had refused to go over and see a manager. Who does that Chadwick think he is?

Well, I had seen refs running over to coaches enough times when I was a linesman to decide that if I ever was a ref in this league I would never demean myself that way. Can you imagine a baseball manager like, say, Leo Durocher, ordering Bill Klem to his dugout because he had something to say to him? It isn't done. It's simply no way to run a hockey game and I had decided a long time before that I'd never do it.

There was one fight in that game between Pat Egan of the Amerks and Bill Juzda of the Rangers. Not a big thing, but enough of a bout to keep things interesting. I also had a strict rule of thumb for fights. Often I'd yell to my linesman, "Let them go." I'm a firm believer that many players fight because they figure it'll be stopped. So, unless it was a mismatch, I didn't hurry in to stop it. That way, maybe those two guys wouldn't be so anxious to go at it again the next time they met.

I always looked for the player who threw the first punch, too. It might only be a glancing blow, and the other player, who, let us say, was completely innocent, swung back and thrashed the aggressor. In a case like that, the player who tossed the first punch would get a major five-minute penalty and the man who defended himself and may even have won the fight, would get only two minutes for swinging back.

I somehow survived my first game and my trial by fire with Red Dutton, who, by the way, wound up happy since the Americans beat the Rangers, 4-1, that night. I must have done the right thing, too, because the next day the headline over Jim Burchard's story of the game in the New York *World-Telegram* read, "GREEN REFEREE TURNS HIS BACK ON DUTTON." Burchard's story said I had speeded up the game by ignoring Dutton's request for a midgame conversation.

Five weeks after the 1941 National Hockey League season started, Japan bombed Pearl Harbor, plunging the United States into World War II. And when America went to war, so did the NHL and its hard-nosed new referee from New York. It took about three months for Uncle Sam to catch up with me, but in March 1942, I got my induction notice. The greetings ordered me to Grand Central Palace located at Grand Central Station, which served as an induction center.

Now I'm as patriotic as the next guy and let me tell you, three months after Pearl Harbor this whole country was one sea of patriotism. But that induction notice had come at the worst possible time for me. The NHL was in the midst of the playoffs, and that was no time for a referee to go marching off to the army. I asked for a two-week extension on my physical and subsequent induction. Those two weeks would allow me to complete the playoffs and earn maybe $1,000. And in 1942, $1,000 was an awful lot of money to pass up. So I went to the draft board and requested the delay.

A few days later the answer came from my draft board. It was a two-word reply to my two-week request. "Request denied," said the draft board.

Now I had made no secret about my request. News of it had been printed all around the league. In Detroit, Lew Walter's story was headlined, "ONE-EYED REFEREE ASKS TWO-WEEK DEFERMENT." It was the first time my disability was brought to the public's attention that way, and I can't say I was thrilled about it.

After the draft board turned down my request, I figured I was gone. So I packed my things, and Millie and I rode the subway from Jamaica to Grand Central Palace. Millie gave me a watch as a going-away present because when you reported for your physical, you were inducted and sent packing the same day.

Nowadays a man blind in one eye wouldn't have to worry about being inducted into the army. But times were different three months after Pearl Harbor. Then, just about everybody was going and I felt that included the one-eyed referee in some shape or form. But I was wrong.

After following the seemingly endless lines of tests and examinations that every army recruit goes through, I reached the last desk, where a sergeant was stationed to stamp the inductee's papers either "Accepted" or "Rejected." When I got there, the desk was manned by a young fellow who glanced at my paper work and then looked up at me.

"Are you Bill Chadwick, the hockey referee?" he asked.

"Yes," I said, nodding. "Why?"

"Aren't you looking for a two-week deferment to handle the playoffs?"

Again I nodded.

"Well I'm Hype Igoe's son," said the sergeant. "I'll get you your two weeks." He took the papers and stamped them, "Insufficient blood tests. Rejected."

"See you in two weeks, Chadwick," he said.

Hype Igoe was a boxing writer for the New York *Journal-American*, and while I never knew him, the fraternity of sports and fate got me those two weeks I wanted so desperately. I refereed in the playoffs, and after they were over, I returned for what I again figured would be my induction at Grand Central Palace.

Again I went through the whole routine from one test to another until I finally reached that last desk where the sergeant with the magic stamp determined your future. This time the sergeant wasn't Hype Igoe's son. When my turn came, I stepped up to his desk. He shuffled through my papers for a few moments.

"Chadwick," he said. "You're blind in one eye. Is that right?"

I nodded.

"That would mean restricted duty then," said the sergeant. "Our limited service quota has been filled for the day."

And with that, the sergeant stamped my papers "Rejected." For the second time in a month, I had packed my bags, prepared to go off to the army, and wound up back home in Jamaica with Millie. For me at least, it was two strikes and out—out of the war.

6
GOOD-BYE, DETROIT

My first season as a referee in the NHL, 1941–1942, was the last one in the league for Red Dutton's Amerks. There had been a last-ditch effort to instill interest in the club by naming them the Brooklyn Americans and having the team practice at the old Brooklyn Ice Palace.

Dutton moved to Flatbush with his wife and tried to get most of his players apartments there, too, in an effort to develop civic pride in Brooklyn's own team. It didn't work, but not for lack of effort on Dutton's part. Red was always thinking of the angles, always looking for a little bit of an edge if he could get one. I learned that early in my first season during a game between the Americans and the Chicago Black Hawks.

Paul Thompson, who, like Dutton, was a westerner and a good hockey player in his time, was coach of the Black Hawks. He was in his fourth season, which was something of a longevity record for Major McLaughlin.

On this particular night Thompson's Black Hawks were beating the Amerks' brains out. That wasn't especially unusual because the Americans were a terrible team and were quite used to losing badly—even to Chicago, which wasn't exactly a powerhouse either.

Anyway, after the second period Dutton came parading into my dressing room. That was standard operating procedure for managers and coaches. They made that room seem like Grand Central Terminal during the rush hour, tramping in and out to cry and moan over this call or that one. Sometimes, there would actually be a line outside that room with one club official waiting for another one to finish his griping. It was just another form of the constant intimidation of officials that went on.

Well, in marched Dutton, thumbing through his tattered copy of the NHL rule book. "Hey, rook," he said, beginning our conversation with the usual cordial greeting reserved for this first-year referee, "you got a tape measure?"

I smiled at him. "I always have one, Mr. Dutton," I said.

"Well, get it out," said Dutton, "because I want you to measure LoPresti's pads."

Sam LoPresti was the Chicago goalie, and like me, he was an American. He was from Eveleth, Minnesota, home of Boston's Frankie Brimsek, another very good NHL goalie.

The NHL rule book says that a goalie's pads must not measure more than ten inches across. This is one of those unenforceable rules because even if a goalie's pads start the game at ten inches in width, there's no way they can stay that way. A goalie bounces up and down on his pads so often that they're bound to spread in the course of the game. And then there's the habit all goalies seem to have of pounding on their pads with their sticks. This also tends to flatten and widen the pads.

Dutton knew that by the third period LoPresti's pads would have to be wider than the prescribed ten inches. That's why he demanded that I measure them. He also knew that as soon as Paul Thompson saw me measure LoPresti's pads the Chicago coach would demand that I measure Earl Robertson's pads. So as soon as we got back to the ice, Dutton called his goalie, Robertson, over to the Americans' bench and instructed him not to pound on his pads with his stick.

When I hit the ice, I called LoPresti over to the penalty box for the measurement. He was totally bewildered by my summons.

"What's up, Bill?" he asked.

"Put your leg up here," I said, taking the tape measure out of my pocket.

By that time Dutton and Thompson were on the scene to watch the measurement. I stretched the tape across LoPresti's pads, and sure enough they measured 10¼ inches—one-quarter inch over the allowed width.

That was all Dutton had to see. He flung his hat in the air and started waving his arms, all the time yelling, "Protest . . . protest!" Well, it didn't take long for the Chicago Stadium fans to start some hooting and hollering of their own. Pretty soon we were on the verge of a rather nasty scene.

There seemed to be only one man in the whole building who wasn't excited—besides me, of course. That was Paul Thompson, the Chicago coach. Thompson was as calm as could be.

"Bill," he said, "call Robertson over and measure his pads."

I beckoned Robertson over to our little conference and pulled out my tape again. I stretched it across the goalie's pad. And what do you think we found? Robertson's pads measured 10½ inches—a full half-inch over the maximum allowed and a quarter of an inch more in violation of the rule than LoPresti's were.

Well, Dutton just about blew a fuse. He was so mad there seemed to be steam escaping from both his ears. And while Red was sputtering and fuming, Thompson was doubling over in gales of laughter. Paul couldn't stop laughing, and I can just imagine what must have happened after the game when Thompson and Dutton got together for a little refreshment.

It might sound strange that rival coaches would wind up drinking together after a hockey game, but that's the way it was. I even know some referees who might bend an elbow or two after a rough game. One of those who didn't, however, was my friend King Clancy. Now Clancy might act like he had a load on, but I'm here to tell you that the King never sipped anything stronger than Coca-Cola.

Clancy is the world's greatest character. If you ask me, he was the Babe Ruth of hockey. He did it all in this game. He was a top-notch player, one hell of a referee, and a successful coach and front-office administrator, too. Besides that, he's just plain fun to be around. King has a way of putting a smile into life's darkest moments. It's his Irish sense of humor, I guess.

Clancy had played many years for the Toronto Maple Leafs and rejoined that organization after his refereeing days were over. Being the outgoing, warm kind of guy that he is, Clancy was able to make many friends in the city of Toronto. But just because they were his friends, that didn't prevent the people from ganging up on King when he made what they considered a bad call against the Maple Leafs.

One night in Maple Leaf Gardens one of Clancy's pals had a front-row seat. The man was a doctor, well-known in the city of Toronto, and a good friend of King. Early in the game Clancy collared a couple of Leafs for what the good doctor considered questionable penalties. That started the dialogue, which, for a long while, was one way.

"Clancy, open your blankety-blank eyes," bellowed the doctor.

"Get in the game, will you, King."

"This is a good game, Clancy. You ought to watch it."

"When's the last time you had your eyes examined, King?"

This went on for a while, and Clancy, who is the world's best-natured guy, shrugged off the complaints. But the doctor didn't get tired. He stayed on King's back for the better part of two periods. Finally, Clancy grew weary of listening to the incessant heckling. Early in the third period there was a whistle and a pause in the play. King took advantage of the break to skate by his friend's seat. He stopped for a moment.

"You know, doctor," said Clancy, "I make an awful lot of mistakes."

"I know, I know," answered the doctor, gleefully.

"But there's one thing about my mistakes, doctor," Clancy continued.

"What's that?" asked the heckler.

"I don't bury mine!"

And with that, Clancy skated away. He didn't hear from the doctor for the rest of the night.

That reminds me of something Mickey Ion told me when I was breaking into the NHL. I had lined a game that Ion was refereeing and there was an awful commotion over some of his calls. The fans were ranting and raving and raising all hell. But Ion didn't seem the least bit disturbed. After the game I asked him how he stayed so cool.

"When things get like that," Ion told me, "I remind myself that there are 14,000 people in the building and that I'm the only one of them who's sane."

The Rangers finished in first place in my first season of refereeing in the NHL and had three of the league's top four scorers in Bryan Hextall, who finished first in the scoring race; Lynn Patrick, who was second; and Phil Watson, who was fourth. Hextall totaled 56 points, which would hardly get him in the top 20 by today's standards.

There were seven teams in the league and six of them qualified for the playoffs. Only Red Dutton's poor old Americans, who had finished last, were out of it. In the first round the Rangers and the Leafs, who had finished second, played a best-of-seven series. Meanwhile the third- and fourth-place clubs, Boston and Chicago, and the fifth- and sixth-place clubs, Detroit and Montreal, played three-game series.

Toronto beat the Rangers in six games to qualify for the Stanley Cup finals. Boston eliminated Chicago, and Detroit beat Montreal. Then the Red Wings beat Boston to qualify for the finals against the Maple Leafs.

Naturally, Toronto, which had finished second during the regular season, was favored to beat Detroit, which had finished in fifth place, closer to the last-place Americans than they were to the second-place Maple Leafs.

Clancy refereed the first game of the series, and the Red Wings, with Don Grosso scoring two goals, beat the Leafs, 3-2. I was up next and again Grosso scored twice and again Detroit stunned Toronto, 4-2. The third-game refereeing assignment went to Norm Lamport, and amazingly, the Red Wings won again, this time by a 5-2 score.

The hockey world was amazed at what was happening. The Red Wings had Toronto on the run. They needed only one more victory to clinch the Stanley Cup. Detroit went for the knockout at home, and in the gloomy Toronto dressing room, bench-warmer Billy Taylor offered a prediction. "Don't worry about us," Taylor told reporters, who were inquiring about how it felt to be on the very edge of elimination. "We'll beat them four straight."

Mel Harwood refereed the fourth game and it was an awful mess. Toronto won it, 4-3, but the game ended in a near riot. A couple of Detroit players, Eddie Wares and Don Grosso, were unhappy with some penalties Harwood had doled out to them. Wares refused to leave the ice and wound up with a misconduct penalty and a $50 fine. Grosso threw down his stick and gloves and offered to fight—a little act that cost him $25. Then Jack Adams, general manager-coach of the Red Wings, rushed onto the ice at the final buzzer and actually did get into a fight with Harwood. That measure of sportsmanship gave Adams an indefinite suspension by the president of the league, Frank Calder. I would have thrown the bum out of hockey, if I'd had my way.

Clancy drew the fifth-game assignment and again Toronto staved off elimination, battering Detroit, 9-3, with Don Metz getting three goals and Syl Apps adding two. Bob Goldham of the Leafs and Detroit's Grosso got into a slugging match and the game was generally chippy, keeping Clancy quite busy.

It was my turn for game six, and I was worried over what might happen after the riotous fourth and fifth games. This time, though, the players stuck to hockey and I didn't have to hand out any penalties. Toronto goalie Turk Broda, always a great playoff competitor, shut out the Red Wings and the Leafs won, 3-0, deadlocking the series at three games each and sending it down to one winner-take-all seventh game.

Calder called a meeting before the seventh game with Clancy, Lamport, and me. We talked for a while about what had happened in the series so far, Adams' behavior, and the brawling that had gone on. I figured that he'd assign his senior referee, Clancy, for the seventh game, or else Lamport, who had worked the third game. Calder was almost through with the meeting when he turned to me.

"Bill, I want you to ref the seventh game," he said.

I was stunned. A seventh-game Cup assignment was unheard of for a rookie referee. And consecutive Cup assignments were also most unusual. But Calder was breaking with tradition on both counts. Even though I was a rookie, and even though I had refereed the sixth game, he sent me back in the box again.

Maple Leaf Garden was absolutely packed for the game. The crowd of 16,218 was the largest ever to see a game in Canada and they were absolutely howling. As the screams rang in my ears, I remembered the motto Mickey Ion had operated by and decided that I was the only sane person in the building.

Sweeney Schriner, one of Red Dutton's old Americans, scored two goals for the Leafs, and Toronto won the game,

3-1, and the Cup, four games to three. The victory climaxed one of the most incredible hockey comebacks ever—a feat that has never been matched. Here was a team with no margin for error, one defeat away from elimination, that came back to win the whole ball of wax. And do you know who fed Schriner the puck and earned the assist on the insurance goal? Why, Billy Taylor, who had predicted the comeback.

Giving me that important seventh-game playoff assignment was one of Calder's last official acts as president of the NHL. Midway through the next season, he suffered a heart attack and died. As his replacement, the NHL Board of Governors selected Red Dutton, whose Americans had suspended operation.

I had to laugh at Dutton's selection. Here was one of the game's best referee-baiters, a man who had a knack for creeping right under a ref's skin. And now he was our boss, president of the league, and, I suppose, the defender of the referees. However, I soon found out how much defense I could expect from him.

The 1943-1944 season belonged to the Montreal Canadiens, who lost only five games all year and finished first, 25 points ahead of Detroit. The Canadiens had a powerhouse team with goalie Bill Durnan leading the league with a 2.18 goals-against average and shooters like Elmer Lach, Toe Blake, and a youngster named Maurice (the "Rocket") Richard providing plenty of scoring.

Naturally, Montreal was favored in the playoffs, and they didn't disappoint their backers, eliminating Toronto in the first round in just five games. Meanwhile, Chicago, which had finished fourth and had lost more games than it had won during the regular season, pulled a shocker. The Black Hawks stunned Detroit, the second-place club, and knocked off the Red Wings in five games.

That set up a Stanley Cup final between the Canadiens and Black Hawks, and the Chicago fans were so excited by their surprising semifinal victory over Detroit that they were convinced the Hawks would knock off the Canadiens and walk off with the Cup. Montreal, of course, had other ideas.

. The series began in Montreal, and King Clancy drew the refereeing assignment for the first game. The Canadiens won, 5-1, and now the series moved to Chicago for the second game. Since Clancy and I handled just about all the playoffs ourselves, that meant it was my turn to handle game two. My linesmen were Jim Primeau, whose brother, Joe, had played for Toronto, and Ed Mepham.

Maurice Richard had scored two goals, and the Canadiens were holding a 2-1 lead in the third period. Richard and his linemates—Lach and Blake—were on the ice and attacking in Chicago's end of the ice. One of the Hawks' defensemen was a guy named George Allen, and he was all tangled up with Lach in front of the Black Hawks' net.

Allen started yelling, "Hold! Hey, Chadwick, he's holding me." He got so excited that he broke away from Lach and chased over to me, ranting and waving his arms. Instead of waiting for The Big Whistle to blow his whistle and assess a penalty, Allen started arguing.

Well, that was his prerogative, to argue like that. And it was my prerogative not to call the holding or to blow my whistle. Allen exercised his prerogative and I exercised mine. And while he was standing there squawking at me, Lach was free in front of the net. Leaving Lach free to roam was a mistake. Sure enough, he got the puck over to Richard and the Rocket put it in the Hawks' net for his third goal of the game.

It wasn't easy to see Richard's goal with Allen standing right in front of me, arguing, instead of covering Lach, but I just caught a glimpse of the goal over Allen's shoulder. When the red goal light went on, I thought that crowd was going to tear old Chicago Stadium down, brick by brick.

"No, no, no," Allen kept repeating over and over, following me around the ice. And my answer was just as brief. "Yes, yes, yes," I said. Richard's goal counted.

The fans went slightly crazy. They began throwing things. At first it was the usual coins—always copper, never silver—and then it advanced to more esoteric things like cigarette lighters, keys, nuts and bolts, and yes, even a pair of false teeth. In a case like that there's no place for a hockey referee to hide. So I went to center ice and stationed myself as far away from the stands as I could.

After they finished with whatever they had in their pockets, the fans started throwing rubbers and boots and even chairs at me. It really got scary. I was standing in the middle of a pretty awful mess when I beckoned Jim Primeau, my linesman, over to the center ice circle.

"Jim," I said, "Dutton's sitting over there in a box seat. Go ask him what I should do."

Primeau was safe because he hadn't done anything as far as the fans were concerned. I was the culprit. I was the guy they were throwing things at. Jim skated over to Dutton's box and delivered my message. I could see Red bending over, listening to Primeau, nodding his head. Then I saw him answering my question, gesturing for emphasis. He'll bail me out, I thought.

Now Primeau skated back to center ice, where I was waiting anxiously.

"Well, what did he say?" I asked.

"Dutton says," reported Primeau, "you got yourself into this. Now get yourself out of it."

Thank you, Mr. Dutton.

I should have known better than to ask Dutton, the old referee-baiter, for advice. I'd have gotten as much help from one of the gallery gods. The demonstration went on for maybe 10 or 15 minutes, but it seemed much longer to me since I was the butt of the concerted attack. Eventually, they got tired and

I was able to get the ice cleared and the game resumed. But I must say, that was the greatest barrage of garbage I ever had to skate through.

Game three of the series took place three nights later also in Chicago, and Dutton, operating from the safety of his office, directed that he would not tolerate any repetition of the second-game demonstration. He said that if it happened again, he would order the game forfeited. It was an easy order to issue when there weren't 17,000 people sitting around you pegging things at your referee.

Because we alternated assignments, the third game was Clancy's turn to referee. The Black Hawks alerted the city to the problem, and there was a fleet of garbage trucks stationed in front of Chicago Stadium. As the fans filed into the arena, they were stopped and relieved of their garbage. They filled up two or three trucks with the junk and fortunately for Clancy there was no problem. The Canadiens won quietly.

I drew the fourth game and the Canadiens finished the Black Hawks off to clinch the Stanley Cup. But Chicago hockey fans have long memories. From that time on for a good year or so I had to have a police escort in and out of the building. I would be picked up at the Stevens Hotel and brought to the arena by a patrol car. Then, after the game, the police would take me out of the arena.

The next spring, when it came time for the playoffs, I got one of my very biggest kicks in hockey. Montreal and Toronto were meeting in the opening round, and when I got to Montreal, the headline over Elmer Ferguson's story read, "CHADWICK TO REFEREE CANADIEN-LEAF SERIES." It was as if they were advertising my appearance and it just tickled me to see it.

"I am naming the referees publicly," Dutton told the papers, "because I don't believe I have anything to hide. Up to the time I took over, and without casting reflections on anyone, it was the custom to conceal the names of the referees in big games, until they went on the ice. The supposition was, I imagine, that if the names became known in advance, some-one might approach King Clancy or Bill Chadwick or any other referee now on the staff of this league with a crooked proposition. Why, the crook would be carved to ribbons right away. I have nothing to hide, nothing to be ashamed of, noth-ing to conceal about the names of my referees. They are part of the playoff background. Folks want to know who they are and I am here to tell those folks, who are entitled to know."

It was nice to see Dutton so proud of his officials and willing to stand behind them. It's a shame he chose to stand so far behind me when those Chicago fans started throwing all that garbage at me the year before.

The Canadiens were the powerhouse of the league again that season. They were defending Cup champions and had finished first, losing only 8 of 50 games during the regular sea-son, so naturally, they were favored to repeat in the playoffs. Toronto, though, wasn't impressed.

Frank McCool played airtight goal and Ted Kennedy produced the game's only score as the Leafs won the opener, 1-0. Then Toronto came right back and won the second game, 3-2, with McCool again the dominant factor. That sent the Leafs home with a commanding two-game lead in the best-of-seven series.

Montreal took game three at Toronto, 4-1, but Gus Bod-nar's overtime goal gave the Leafs the fourth game, 4-3. That left the Canadiens on the brink of elimination, but they weren't through yet. Rocket Richard scored four goals and Montreal blitzed McCool, 10-3, to win the fifth game. But the Leafs bounced right back to kayo Montreal, 3-2, in game six, eliminating the regular season champions from the Cup com-petition.

Meanwhile, Detroit and Boston went the full seven games in the other semifinal series before the Red Wings finally won it. Carl Liscombe scored four goals as Detroit took the seventh and deciding game, 5-3.

That put the Red Wings and Maple Leafs in the Stanley

Cup finals—a rematch of the Cup showdown my first year in the league when Detroit won the first three games and then Toronto came back to take four in a row and the title. And, believe it or not, this one was almost an instant replay—in reverse.

This time Toronto won the first three games, and they were three tremendous defensive battles. Detroit never scored a goal against the Leafs' cool Frank McCool. He shut them out, 1-0, on a goal by Sweeney Schriner in the first game, beat them, 2-0, with Ted Kennedy and Moe Morris scoring in the second game, and then blanked them again, 1-0, on a goal by Gus Bodnar in game three.

Clancy and I were alternating the games and Dutton was traveling with us. When the Leafs moved to within one victory of finishing off Detroit, the three of us had an added passenger in our bedroom on the Canadian Pacific Railway. We had to have the Stanley Cup on hand for presentation in case the series ended, and the simplest way for it to get to each game was for it to travel with us.

We lugged the mug to Toronto for the fourth game, but Detroit wasn't ready to die. Ted Kennedy scored three goals for the Leafs but the Red Wings solved McCool for five and won, 5-3.

That meant we had to return to Detroit for a fifth game and through customs again with our friend, Stanley Cup. I refereed that game and McCool and Detroit's Harry Lumley put on quite a goaltending duel. It was scoreless until the third period, when Flash Hollett finally hit for the Red Wings and then Joe Carveth added another goal for a 2-0 victory.

Now it was back to Toronto for game six, Dutton, Clancy, and Chadwick literally lugging old Stanley Cup over the border again. And again, it was a defensive struggle. We had 60 minutes of scoreless hockey with Clancy on top of every play as McCool and Harry Lumley matched save for save. Finally, 14 minutes into the first overtime, Mud Bruneteau scored the goal that won it for Detroit and tied the series at three games each. Of course, overtime goals were not exactly new for Bruneteau. He had scored the goal that ended the longest game in NHL history, a six-overtime struggle between the Red Wings and Montreal Maroons that began on March 24, 1936, and ended early the next morning.

Anyway, Bruneteau's overtime goal tied the series and back we went to Detroit—Dutton, Clancy, Chadwick, and the Cup. The customs man was so used to seeing us, he didn't even ask about the big, wooden case in which we were carting hockey's most treasured trophy. There was one nice thing about the trip to Detroit for that seventh, final game. We knew that somebody would finally win the Cup and we'd be rid of it once and for all.

It was my turn to referee and I was excited. There is nothing quite like the seventh game of the Stanley Cup finals. Jack Adams and the Red Wings were perfectly happy to have me refereeing that seventh game. I had always had a good press in Detroit and the Red Wing organization praised me frequently. You might have called me the fair-haired boy in Detroit—until that seventh game.

Toronto scored first on a goal by Mel Hill, and McCool protected that lead into the third period. Then Murray Armstrong busted through to score for Detroit and tie the game. Now it became a game of cat-and-mouse with each team waiting for the other to make a mistake—the one mistake that could prove fatal. Finally Detroit's Syd Howe made it. He cross-checked Gus Bodnar behind the net.

There were maybe seven minutes to play and the play was behind Detroit's net when Howe, not to be confused with Gordie, gave Bodnar a good two-hander. The play was right in front of me and I called it.

I raised my arm, pointed at Howe, and blew the whistle. "Howe! I want you. Two minutes for cross-checking."

"No, Bill," bellowed Howe. "No!"

"You're gone, Syd," I answered.

There was a moan from the crowd as Howe headed for

the penalty box, and on the Red Wing bench Jack Adams was absolutely livid. He called me some awful things but nothing I hadn't been called before in rinks from the Brooklyn Ice Palace to River Vale, New Jersey, to Madison Square Garden, to Chicago Stadium. It all rolled right off my back as the players lined up for Toronto's power play.

The Leafs won the drop and rushed into Detroit's end. They worked the puck around, looking for the open man, trying to set up that one good shot. Finally the puck came to the point and there was Babe Pratt, an economy-sized Toronto defenseman, waiting for it. Pratt lined up the puck and shot it low and hard and true.

The puck zipped under goalie Harry Lumley and into the Red Wings' net. The Maple Leafs led, 2-1, and that was enough for McCool. He made the lead stand up the rest of the way and the Leafs won the game and the Cup, putting a halt to Detroit's determined comeback.

Afterward, Adams made a point of paying me a social visit to my dressing room, where he called me every name he could think of because I had the audacity to call a cross-checking penalty on one of his guys with so little time left to play.

What really bothered Adams was that it had happened in the Detroit Olympia, the Red Wings' home ice. How could I call a penalty like that on the home team?

My answer was simple. A cross-check is a cross-check, no matter who does it and no matter what building he does it in. That answer turned Adam's tomato-shaped face a deep shade of red, and he questioned my ancestry in strong terms.

That was the beginning of my falling out of favor with the Detroit organization. From that day on Adams and the Red Wings made a career of riding the ass off Bill Chadwick. And do you know something? That may very well have been the very best thing that ever happened to me.

7
RATING THE BRASS

James Norris, Sr., was owner of the Detroit Red Wings hockey club and, he thought, just about everything else in the National Hockey League. Pop Norris, as he was called, had interests in both the Chicago Stadium, where the Black Hawks played, and Madison Square Garden, home of the New York Rangers. That accounted for half of the six teams in the National Hockey League, so maybe Pop Norris was right when he thought he owned the league.

Anyway, losing never sat well with Pop, and after every game he'd be on the telephone with his general manager-coach, Jack Adams. And every time, the conversation would center around what a lousy job the referee had done. And you can just imagine the conversation when Adams told Norris about the penalty I had given Syd Howe in the final minutes of the seventh game of the playoffs. After that, Norris and Adams pledged to get me out of the NHL, and I think that's the one thing that kept me in the league for as long as I lasted. The rest of the league came to my defense and I guess psychologically they must have felt that if Detroit and Norris were so dead set against Chadwick, why then, he must have something for the rest of us, so we'll be for him.

I'm sure that many times through the years those other clubs had reservations about their support of me, but overall they were behind me because Detroit was against me. They shoved me down the throats of Norris and Adams, and I'm sure it left a terrible aftertaste. Detroit couldn't get me out of the league because of my refereeing ability. Also, I couldn't be intimidated, no matter how many coaches, general managers, and/or owners paraded in and out of my dressing room before, during, and after hockey games. That was another thing, I think, that bugged Norris and his errand boy, Adams.

Norris was used to getting his way, and so he began trying to force me out of the league. When he found resistance from the other owners on a straightforward dismissal of Chadwick, he did a natural thing for him: He turned devious.

On my first trip into Montreal the following season I was summoned to the league office. Clarence Campbell, who had replaced Dutton as president, met me. We spent a few minutes in polite small talk, but I knew there was something on Campbell's mind and that he hadn't called me in to discuss the weather. Finally he got to the point.

"Bill," he said, "one of the owners in the league has requested that you go to McGill University for an eye test."

Now Campbell knew I had lost my right eye many years before and so did every coach, general manager, and owner in the league. But fortunately for me, my left eye had 20-20 vision. I suspected immediately that the owner making the request was my buddy, Norris, and shortly afterwards that hunch was confirmed.

From that time on, every year, as regular as clockwork, on my first trip into Montreal, I was instructed to go to McGill for an eye test. It became part of my start-of-season routine, and it never really bothered me because I'm smug enough to believe I could have refereed just as well—no, make that better—than anybody else, just from memory. Now you might get some contradiction on that point from my friends, the coaches, but I think overall that my record speaks for itself.

Ah, the coaches. They were a classic bunch and ran the gauntlet from Adams, who was one of the greatest coaches ever to sit on the end of a bench in the National Hockey League, to Chicago's Johnny Gottselig, who didn't know which end of the stick was up.

Adams had a marvelous record of achievement with the Red Wings, but that doesn't change my feelings about the man. He is far and away at the bottom of my personal list. He was the master of intimidation—not only with referees but also with his own players. At that time the Red Wings' chief farm club was Indianapolis, and Adams would carry a stack of round-trip tickets between the two cities with him all the time. If a man didn't produce, Adams wasted no time. He'd hand him a ticket to Indianapolis right there in the dressing room. Nice guy.

After Adams gave up the coaching job with Detroit, he remained as general manager and hired Tommy Ivan to run the team from the bench. But that wasn't entirely true either, because every game that Ivan coached the Red Wings, Adams sat one row behind the bench with Mrs. Adams, always more than willing to offer some advice.

Ivan had been a scout for the Red Wings and was a short, frail-looking guy compared to big, blustery Jack Adams. They were quite a study in contrasts. Ivan couldn't get out from under Adams' thumb until he moved on to the Chicago organization as general manager. It was only then that he really became his own man.

In Chicago, Major McLaughlin's revolving door for coaches seemed stuck on Paul Thompson when I got to the NHL. Thompson was a happy-go-lucky fellow whose brother, Tiny Thompson, was a first-rate goalie for Boston. Paul succeeded my old friend Bill Stewart as Chicago's coach in 1938–1939 and was a pleasant guy on the bench. He hassled the referee only when he thought he was being dealt with unfairly and you don't mind hearing from guys like him.

Thompson stayed on as coach of the Black Hawks until

1944-1945 when Johnny Gottselig took over. That was a laugh. Of any coach on the NHL scene in the years I refereed, I had the least amount of respect for Gottselig. He turned up later as the Black Hawks' public relations man and I think he did a terrible job there, too. He also did some broadcasting and he wasn't very good at that either.

Charley Conacher followed Gottselig, and I always had a soft spot in my heart for him. I liked him a lot. He was a rough, tough character and a good friend of King Clancy's which meant he was also a friend of mine. Sid Abel followed Conacher and he also served as a general manager later in Detroit when Adams finally faded from the picture.

Possibly the best coach in the league when I was refereeing was Dick Irvin in Montreal. He was everything you'd want in a coach. He lived, ate, and slept hockey. He was also the cleanest coach in the league because he continually filled his pockets with cakes of soap from the hotels where the Canadiens stopped. Irvin was a great hockey man and his record confirms it. He also had some pretty good material to work with. It's not half-bad when you can put together lines like Toe Blake, Elmer Lach, Maurice Richard, and later Bert Olmstead, defensemen like Ken Reardon and Butch Bouchard, and a goalie like Bill Durnan. Every one of those guys except Olmstead is in the Hockey Hall of Fame, and I imagine Bert will make it someday, too.

But there were times in the very beginning when I first got into the league that Montreal wasn't that great. The man who turned them around was Dick Irvin.

Toronto had some great coaching staffs until, of course, they got to my friend Clancy. No, not really. I'm only kidding about King. All you have to do is look at the record to find out the kind of job he did whenever the Maple Leafs needed him in a pinch. One year, when Punch Imlach developed an ulcer from watching the Leafs lose a dozen or so games in a row, they carted him off to the hospital and handed the job to

Clancy. The Leafs promptly turned right around and won ten straight for King. He had the same kind of success more recently when John McLellan was sidelined by stomach trouble. And I know that if the Leafs ever send their current coach, Red Kelly, off to the hospital, Clancy will be available to put them back together again.

When I came into the league, Hap Day was the Toronto coach. He was an outstanding hockey man. He knew the game in and out and was a great psychologist. In his own way he could intimidate you every bit as well as the old master, Jack Adams, but at least he was more pleasant about it.

Then came Joe Primeau, who like Day, wound up in the Hall of Fame. Clancy followed them, and I maintain that King stands as the Babe Ruth of hockey. He's done so much for this game in every capacity. He also happens to be a great guy and the best friend I ever had in this game.

Cooney Weiland was Boston's coach when I got to the NHL and while he was a great hockey player, I just don't think he was much of a coach in this league. He later went on to coach at Harvard and was quite successful at the collegiate level of hockey.

Later came Art Ross, who had a good feeling for the game and protected it from some of the egomaniacs who were masquerading as owners during those years. Then, for a time, two great players, Dit Clapper and Milt Schmidt, served as coaches. It's hard for me to assess them as coaches because I have so much respect for them as individuals. They were both the same type of guys—both great hockey players and both would be on my team if I were putting one together to play in the NHL.

In New York, Ross had an ally in Lester Patrick, who also recognized what a great game hockey could become provided it could survive the showboats who were running the league and most of its clubs. Lester was the Rangers' first coach, but he had moved upstairs to the general manager's job by the time I got to the NHL. Then Frank Boucher, one of the Rangers' original star players under Patrick, was coach of the club. But Boucher was no Patrick. For a while the momentum of Lester's era carried the Rangers, but Boucher could not maintain it.

Then Lynn Patrick, Lester's son, became coach. Lynn did as good a job as was possible with the material he inherited from Boucher. That wasn't a whole lot. Boucher, in my opinion, will not be remembered as a great coach. But he was the man who turned hockey around with the introduction of the red line.

Before the red line, the rule book said that a team had to carry the puck out of its own zone. What would happen is that a team would be jammed in its own end for minutes on end. It was next to impossible for the player to stickhandle their way out with five enemy players to get around. Boucher's idea was to permit a pass out and the red line was used to indicate how far that pass could travel without penalty. When the league put in that red line, it speeded up the game and started what is recognized as hockey's modern era.

After that, the Rangers went into a period where they were floundering and shifting coaches almost every year. They used Alf Pike, Neil Colville, Phil Watson, and Muzz Patrick. But the team never jelled until the mid-sixties, a good ten years after I had retired as a referee, when Emile Francis took over.

There was one particularly melancholy time when the club was so bad on the ice that they tried gimmicks. They had a New York restaurant owner fix up a special elixir that was supposed to make them winners. Then they hired a hypnotist. None of that junk did anything to change what was happening on the ice, and believe me, that was pretty bad. They couldn't beat that old vaudeville team Singer's Midgets.

Now if you thought the coaches were a collection of strange sorts, you should have seen the general managers and owners. Of course, being a referee, I saw all of them all the time. Even when I didn't want to. Adams was a perfect example. He was always in our dressing room between periods telling us what a bad game we were calling. That crap went on for five years until finally the NHL made a rule about it. They ordered Mr. Adams to knock before walking into the room.

A process of intimidation was always there in one way or another. And it never ended. Even during the off-season, the line was drawn. Management was on one side of it and the referees in general and Chadwick in particular were on the other side.

A referee's life can be a lonely one, and each season I'd be away from home for days and sometimes even weeks at a time. As we hit playoff time, I began to anticipate the end of the season when I could finally see my family again. April was always a big month in our house because Millie and I celebrate our anniversary that month and both our children, Barbara and Billy, were born in that month, too. So April was always a sort of Christmas for us. Every season, after I got home, we tried to go away for a while on vacation just to get to know the family again and to recuperate from the long season.

One April we went down to Bermuda for our postseason vacation. We were there a couple of days when we decided to go into Hamilton to do a little shopping. Millie and I strolled into a rather large department store and who do we see standing there, bigger than life, but General John Reed Kilpatrick, president of the New York Rangers. General Kilpatrick, who would never be mistaken for Emile Francis or Tommy Ivan, was wearing plaid Bermuda shorts, and if you ever saw the general in plaid Bermuda shorts, you would never forget it.

I walked over to him with my hand out and said, "General, how are you?"

Kilpatrick glared at me and snapped, "How can you have the audacity to talk to me after what you did to the New York Rangers last season?"

Well, if you ever saw a crushed individual, Bill Chadwick was it. At that time I didn't have an answer for the general. At this time I would.

Kilpatrick was more of a fan than he was president of the hockey club. I can see him and his rotund belly bouncing into my dressing room and giving me hell. It happened more than once.

Art Ross was the general manager in Boston, and like Lester Patrick, he thought more of hockey than he did of himself. They were the only ones about whom you could say that. He wanted hockey to be the great game that it eventually turned out to be.

Later, Walter Brown served as the Bruins' general manager and he was very much like Tommy Lockhart, an American who thought progressively about the game and helped in its development. Milt Schmidt also did a stint as general manager later on.

The owner of the Bruins was the Adams family, and they were, like Kilpatrick, just overblown fans.

Tommy Gorman was general manager in Montreal, but the Canadiens didn't become a powerhouse until Frank Selke was brought in to that job. Selke had been an assistant general manager in Toronto, but he had nothing to say there. That changed when he moved to the Canadiens and started Montreal's dynasty. He was a great man for hockey and recognized that it was also a business, not just a sport. In his own way, he did as much for the sport as Clarence Campbell.

The owner of the Canadiens was Senator Donat Raymond, a quiet gentleman who remained in the background. In Toronto, it was all Connie Smythe. The general manager was Connie Smythe. The president was Connie Smythe. And I wouldn't be surprised if the head ticket-taker was also Connie Smythe. He was quite a showman, and in my opinion he should have been part of Barnum and Bailey. He always had a show.

Smythe always prided himself on having the finest arena in the National Hockey League, and it was always the cleanest, too. You could eat off the floor then and you can eat off the floor now. He was an egotist, just like the others, but I think in later years he began to turn the corner and started to think of the National Hockey League as a big-league affair.

I had my share of tough moments in Smythe's Maple Leaf Gardens. You always had him and half of his board of directors helping you out at every game. The Maple Leafs were the first team to film their games. They'd take movies of a game on a Saturday night and then run them Monday morning and criticize the referee. Well, hell, on a Monday anybody can referee a game that was played on Saturday. They'd always invite me to come in and watch their films but I respectfully declined. I wasn't interested in instant replays then and I don't care for them now.

I do believe that Smythe, in his heart, had great respect for me. He showed it in many ways. Once, during the playoffs, the Maple Leafs were playing Detroit in the opening round and the Red Wings were winning the first game by a big margin. I caught Tod Sloan, a Maple Leaf, on a tripping penalty and called it. Sloan wasn't happy with the call and raced at me. He cocked his fist as if he was going to punch me. He never did, but he didn't have to. As soon as he got his fist up there like that, he was gone on a match penalty.

I figured that Smythe would have a few unkind things to say about that call. But much to my surprise, instead of complaining, Smythe said I'd made the right decision. The headline in the Toronto paper the next day told the whole story. "THERE'S NO HOPE LEFT," it read, "SMYTHE PRAISES REFEREE." Not only did he praise me but he went a step further: The next year he traded Sloan to the Black Hawks.

Jack Adams was the general manager and coach in Detroit, and the owner was my benefactor, James Norris, Sr., or, as Adams used to refer to him, Old Man Norris. They were quite a team. I'd love to go back into the files of the National Hockey League some day and see how many letters there were on Detroit Red Wing stationary requesting that I be forcibly retired and leave the hockey scene.

Then you had Chicago, which was an absolute hodge-podge. Bill Tobin was the general manager, but he was nothing more than an errand boy for Major McLaughlin. The major got the Chicago franchise and nicknamed his club the Black Hawks after the regiment he had commanded during World War I.

Major McLaughlin had a coffee business in Chicago, and he married Irene Castle of the famous dance team. The major was quite a character. I can remember him sitting up there in his box seat at Chicago Stadium, and many a time I'd have liked to have creamed him with a puck if I could have thrown it at him. He was a smug individual and he didn't know the first thing about hockey as his teams proved through the years.

One of his bright ideas was to put together an all-American hockey club with no Canadian players on it at all. It was an absolute disaster.

The only time Chicago started to go was when young Jim Norris, the son of the patriarch in Detroit, took over. I always had respect for young Jim and I think he always had respect for me.

I heard recently that Connie Smythe and old Jim Norris used to trade hockey players for racehorses and I believe it. They were both that type of individual.

The president of the league, of course, after Red Dutton, was the Rhodes scholar, Clarence Campbell. In my opinion, the league couldn't have survived without him. He took charge when hockey desperately needed someone to do just that. He showed that bunch of egotists that this was a business they were in, not just a sport and that operated properly it would flourish just like any other business. He had the foresight to see just what a great game they had in their hands.

It took some work, believe me. Nobody could cross those people—the McLaughlins and the Kilpatricks and the Smythes and the Norrises. They all knew as much about hockey as my little daughter did. They thought *they* were the show, not the game. They were only interested in fostering their own egos. This must be a great game to have survived the people who were running it.

As I look down the list of all these people I've mentioned—all the owners, all the managers, all the coaches—there are only two I can't remember seeing in my dressing room at one time or another ready with some unsolicited advice for me.

One was Senator Raymond of the Montreal Canadiens who nobody ever saw or heard from. The other was Irene Castle—and that was because she knew I didn't know how to dance.

8

DETECTIVE NEMO

The late Bill Klem, often hailed as baseball's greatest umpire, liked to claim that he never blew a call. As much as I admired Mr. Klem, I must say that's so much malarkey. No official in any sport has been perfect. We've all blown calls at one time or another, and I'm sure Klem was no exception to that rule. I know I wasn't. And, like almost everything about my career, when I blew one it was a dandy.

My biggest blunder came right in the middle of hockey's showcase—the 1954 Stanley Cup playoffs. Boston was playing the Canadiens in Montreal in the first round and the Bruins were on the attack. I was in the middle of the ice, following the play, when a Canadiens' defenseman—I think it was Doug Harvey—slashed the puck-carrier, Doug Mohns.

It was clearly a penalty and I saw it right away. Up went my arm to signal the infraction and then the damnedest thing happened. I blew my whistle while Boston still had control of the puck.

Section 4, Rule 34B of my favorite reading material, the *NHL Rule Book,* clearly states that when a penalty is committed by a team not in possession of the puck, the referee must allow the other team to complete its play before his whistle.

The team committing the penalty must gain possession of the puck before play is halted. Otherwise, you're penalizing the team that has the puck by blowing the whistle and halting play.

It is a delayed penalty, and often you'll see a team pull its goalie off the ice and substitute a sixth skater in an attempt to score during that situation. They can afford to vacate the net because as soon as the team that committed the penalty touches the puck, the ref blows his whistle and stops play, so there's no danger of having a goal scored against the attacking team.

Well, on this particular occasion, The Big Whistle blew his whistle too soon. Boston still had the puck when I blew it, and wouldn't you know it, at that precise moment Mohns shot the puck under Jacques Plante and into the Canadiens' net. My bungle had not only cost Boston a chance to attack the Montreal net. It had cost the Bruins a goal.

As you can well imagine, Lynn Patrick, coach of the Bruins, was absolutely livid on the Boston bench. His face was turning different colors of the rainbow and he was saying some rather unpleasant things about Millie Chadwick's favorite referee. I understood, though, and I'm sure in his place I would have said the same things.

I had committed the cardinal sin of refereeing. I was so intent on nabbing Harvey for that penalty that I had cost the Bruins the tying goal. I skated over to the Boston bench to apologize to Patrick.

"Lynn," I said. "I made a mistake. I'm sorry. I can't breathe in after blowing the whistle. I know I made a mistake."

Patrick wasn't exactly thrilled with my explanation, especially when Montreal came on to win the game and eliminate the Bruins from the semifinals. After the game was over, Lynn showed up at my dressing room as you might expect. But he didn't have the fire in his eyes you might have expected. I must admit I was kind of surprised at that. But what he said next really impressed me and showed the kind of man Lynn Patrick is.

"Bill," he said, "if you're big enough to admit you made a mistake, I will never criticize you again."

And he never did.

The Forum in Montreal and Toronto's Maple Leaf Gardens were always my two favorite rinks to work in. I never had fan problems in either of those places. I'm smug enough to feel that those people knew their hockey and sensed that I was doing my job correctly.

In the other four rinks—New York's Madison Square Garden, the Olympia in Detroit, Boston Garden, and Chicago Stadium—half the fans didn't know what was going on. They just saw a group of guys skating around in pretty uniforms. To them it was like an ice show with sticks. Chicago could get real rough because they just never controlled the fans and those fans tried it all. You were a sitting duck out there, especially when you had to go down the winding staircase behind the end boards to reach your dressing room.

One of my toughest refereeing situations occurred in Chicago and involved one of the few Americans to play in the NHL, Johnny Mariucci. John played for the Black Hawks and he was a character. He had been an all-American end for the University of Minnesota's football team and sometimes he played his hockey as if he were still on the football field. He was a tough individual who would belt an opponent first and ask questions later.

One night the Hawks were at home against Detroit and Mariucci was doing his thing with Black Jack Stewart, one of the toughest defensemen I've ever seen in the National Hockey League. The two of them were bouncing each other pretty good all night long.

Finally, Stewart and Mariucci had one dandy collision in a corner and bodies and sticks went flying in all directions.

When they both recovered from the belt they had given each other, Stewart and Mariucci began searching for their sticks. They both saw one stick, but not the other, and naturally they both grabbed for the one stick.

Mariucci had one end and Stewart the other, and they were both pulling and tugging away when I spotted them. Since that stick had to belong to one of them, the other would be guilty of holding. So I blew the whistle.

When I tooted, the play stopped and Stewart and Mariucci quit tugging, but both still had a firm grasp on that stick—Mariucci at one end and Stewart at the other. And now, I was right in the middle.

Okay, you blew the whistle, you stupid bugger, I said to myself. Now what are you going to do?

Since all hockey sticks look pretty much alike, my problem was going to be how to determine who belonged to this particular stick. The solution, I decided, would be whose number was penciled on the stick. Most hockey players place their uniform numbers on the knob of the stick for identification purposes. It was my great good fortune that Mariucci and Stewart didn't wear the same number.

I looked at the stick and there was Stewart's number. That meant Mariucci was holding and I gave the call with the usual emphasis. Now since we were in Chicago and since Mariucci was a Black Hawk, everybody in the building except the Red Wings and Stewart started hollering for my scalp.

Mariucci was storming around the ice like a wild man, hooting and hollering at me. I think the reaction of the fans, which was long and loud, egged him on and his reaction had the same effect on them.

I finally got him corralled and pointed toward the penalty box. I felt like a rodeo cowboy rounding up a wild bull. Just as Mariucci stepped into the penalty box, one of my friends in the balcony dropped a deck of cards down on the ice. This was a regular practice in Chicago Stadium whenever the gallery gods disagreed with a call. Usually they'd drop a couple of cards at a time so that a deck could last the full game. But when a call was particularly outrageous, as I guess they thought my call on Mariucci was, that called for the full deck being dropped all at once.

Well, this particular deck of cards landed in front of the penalty box where I was standing and Mariucci was sitting and still muttering about my parentage and anything else he could think of at the moment. He was giving it to me pretty good along with the rest of the Black Hawks when I picked up about half of the cards that had landed on the ice and handed them to Mariucci.

"Here, John," I said, "You can use these for a game of solitaire because you just got ten more minutes for misconduct."

Mariucci was flabbergasted but no more so than Danny Lewicki was in another game at Montreal. I was working the game with my old buddy, Sammy Babcock, as my linesman. Babcock and I went back a long time to the days when he and I skated together on Tommy Lockhart's all-American line with the New York Rovers. Sammy and I were great friends and I always enjoyed working with him.

Lewicki was a rookie in the NHL with Toronto. He had been a tremendously successful junior hockey player and came into the NHL with a big buildup, similar nowadays to kids like Denis Potvin of the Islanders and Tom Lysiak of the Flames. All the publicity and adulation by the fans must have gone to Lewicki's head, because he got a little cocky. One night, though, he picked the wrong guy to get cocky with.

In this particular game Toronto was losing and I was getting an earful from the Maple Leaf bench. I didn't recognize the voice but it was certainly irritating me. Naturally, every time I whirled around toward the Leaf bench, the gabbing would stop. Then, as soon as my back was turned again, I'd start getting the treatment all over again.

I finally got tired of listening to it. I was skating alongside my friend Babcock with my back to the Toronto bench when I decided to nail down once and for all the identity of the talkative Leaf.

"Sam, who is giving it to me off that bench?" I asked Babcock.

"Danny Lewicki," he whispered.

"Okay," I said, nodding.

As play continued, I made it a point to keep my back to the Leaf bench, figuring that sooner or later the loquacious Lewicki would have something to say. I didn't have to wait long.

"You're a stiff, Chadwick," said the shrill voice behind me on the Toronto bench.

With that, I whirled and yelled as loudly as I could: "Lewicki, go!"

My voice has always been really loud and clear, so there was never any doubt about what I had in mind. Everybody in the building knew Lewicki was gone for a misconduct, and if you ever saw a beaten dog going across the ice from the bench to the penalty box, it was Danny Lewicki. It was as if he had been caught with his hand in the cookie jar. The part that amazed him was that I caught him while my back was turned. He must have thought I had eyes in the back of my head. I didn't, though. Just a helpful linesman. Thank you, Sammy Babcock.

The worst thing a referee can have is rabbit ears. I always thought I had a high tolerance for players who performed this game with their mouths instead of their sticks and skates. I had two barometers for canning a player with a loose tongue. The first was whether anybody else besides me could hear what he said. If they did, he was gone. If not, he had a chance to stay. The second was whether he really meant those nasty things he was saying. So I'd ask him what he said. If he repeated it, then I had to believe he meant it, and he was gone.

If a player mouthed off to me and the argument was

strictly between the two of us with no fans or other players hearing it, it was okay. I never lost anything in a conversation like that. But once the referee lets the fans or other players hear him, it gets around like wildfire and your respect is shot.

When I gave a penalty, the rule was that the player penalized had to spend the full term of his penalty off the ice, no matter what happened on the ice. That meant a team on a power play could score three or four goals on a single penalty if it were proficient enough. That's why a penalty was a rather major decision when I gave one. When Montreal became so proficient at the power play that it could score three or four times during a single penalty, they changed the rule. Now a penalized player returns as soon as the other team scores during a power play. That takes some of the weight off the penalty.

There were three referees in the NHL and three distinct refereeing styles. King Clancy let them go out and play the game any way they wanted. He called only the most obvious stuff. George Gravel was a close-to-the-vest guy who called just about anything and everything. I played it down the middle. The teams played accordingly and the referee directed how the game would be played.

Clancy and I have always been close, and often we'd call each other to compare notes. Remember, there were only six cities in the league, so we were never very far apart. I would tell King my problems and he would tell me his. If some players gave him trouble, I watched out for them in games I handled, and he'd do the same for me. The players seemed to realize this. They recognized that once they did something to infuriate Chadwick or Clancy, then they had two referees on the lookout for them.

With only six teams the first four qualified for the playoffs, and that meant two semifinal games per night. Clancy would referee one and I the other. In 1949 Detroit won the regular season race and went up against Montreal in the playoffs with Toronto meeting Boston in the other series.

I was in Montreal for the fourth game of the Red Wing–Canadien series and King had the Bruins in Toronto. The next night, we were to shift series with me going to Boston to pick up game five of that series and Clancy heading for Detroit to work the Red Wings and Canadiens.

We were still traveling around mostly by trains then, and to get from Montreal to Boston, Sammy Babcock and I had to come down through New York and then go back up to Massachusetts. We had a fairly easy game with Detroit beating the Canadiens, 3–1. Afterward, we grabbed a cab to Windsor Station for the ride down to New York.

We arrived in Grand Central Station at 8:00 or 9:00 the next morning, and in between trains I walked over to a newsstand to get a Boston paper. There, plastered across the front page were pictures of hockey players cut to ribbons. The Bruins and Leafs had had themselves a war the night before when Clancy refereed their fourth game.

Babcock and I read the paper on the way up to Boston, and I decided that the Bruins and Leafs weren't going to get away with that kind of monkey business in game five. When we got into town, I called Clancy.

"What happened last night, King?" I asked.

"Oh, Bill," King said, "it was an awful mess. A rough, hockey game, but things just got a little out of hand."

"Okay," I told Babcock, "Sammy, we're gonna give it to them tonight because of what went on with Clancy in Toronto last night." I had a method for dealing with teams when I thought they were going into a game with something other than hockey on their minds. On that kind of night, as soon as I dropped the puck, the first guy that blinked an eyelash was gone.

Sure enough, it didn't take long for somebody to blink an

eyelash. And then someone else, and someone else, too. And everyone of them got whistled down. I was throwing guys off the ice left and right, and before the first period was over, I had called 17 minor penalties, which is an awful lot of eyelash-blinking in any man's league.

After the fifth minor penalty I'd given Toronto's Bill Ezinicki, he kind of frowned and looked at me. "Bill, what the hell are you doing?" he asked.

I knew very well what I was doing, and so did Ezinicki.

"If you were in my position, what would you do?" I asked him.

"The same damn thing," he said, stepping into the penalty box.

Later in that game another Toronto player, Jimmy Thompson, said a no-no to me and was gone for 10 minutes on a misconduct. Thompson was cooling his heels in the box when I was forced up against the boards to avoid a play. I was trying to stay out of the way of the action when, boom, the lights went out.

One of the friendly fans had rolled up a newspaper and whacked me over the top of the head. I went down in a heap, flat out on the ice. After a few minutes the cobwebs began to clear and I got to my feet feeling very much like a fighter who's just been kayoed. I was still shaking my head trying to get myself back together when I saw Jimmy Thompson waving for me to come over to the penalty box.

"That's just what I need now, Thompson to start bitching again," I thought to myself.

But that wasn't what he wanted me for.

"Bill," he said, pointing to one of the fans next to the box, "that's the dirty bastard who hit you over there."

I had the man ejected from Boston Garden, which, even though it isn't exactly the most sophisticated spot in the world, still frowns on fans hitting referees over the head with rolled-up newspapers.

After I got rid of him, I skated past Thompson, "Thanks, Jim," I said.

"That's okay, Bill," said Thompson. "He might have swung that thing at me next."

There was an epilogue to that story. A couple of weeks later, I got a letter from the fan, apologizing for what he had done. That was thoughtful of the guy but it didn't do much for the headache he'd given me.

I guess, in retrospect, you could blame Clancy for the 17 first-period penalties and the bop on the head. If he'd clamped down on those guys the night before in Toronto, I wouldn't have had to do it in Boston. But then, Clancy has gotten me in hot water before and he's even spent some time in it with me. There was, for example, our adventure in Toronto with Detective Nemo.

King, as I've indicated before, is a very gregarious guy, outgoing and friendly. That's one of the lovable things about him. The only thing wrong with it is that sometimes he gets friendly with the wrong people.

One of King's friends in Toronto was a shady character who hung out in the lobby of the Royal York Hotel. Clancy introduced me to the guy and we might have had a drink or two with him. Oops, that is, I might have had a drink or two with him. Clancy never drank. Only Coke for the King.

The guy, as far as King and I were concerned, was nothing more than a hockey fan who liked to spend his time around people from the game. There was never any indication that he was anything more or less than that. We'd talk about the league and the different players and just relax with the guy. He was a pleasant chap and King and I both enjoyed his company.

One night Clancy and I went to Buffalo with Clarence Campbell, president of the NHL, to watch an American Hockey League game and evaluate a young referee who was working the game. We got back to Toronto late that evening and picked up a paper in the lobby of the Royal York. There, splashed across the front page in inch-tall letters, was the headline. It hit Clancy and me right between the eyes. Our friend had been found on a suburban road, murdered.

"My God, Bill!" said Clancy, "Look at that, will you!"

Naturally, we were both shocked. A few minutes later, we got another shock. Two detectives from the Toronto police department showed up at the hotel. They had found our names in the guy's wallet and we were wanted for questioning at police headquarters.

All of the color drained out of Clancy's face when the detectives identified themselves and told us about the man's wallet. He was petrified, and frankly, so was I.

"Whatinhell do you want with us?" asked Clancy. "We hardly knew the guy."

"Just come along," said the cop, sounding like something out of a television show. "We want to ask you a few questions."

I looked at King and he looked at me. We were both incredulous, but there wasn't much we could do except go along with the law. But both of us could just imagine the headline in the morning: "TWO NHL REFS IMPLICATED IN MURDER." Lovely.

All the way to the police headquarters Clancy and I kept repeating that we hardly knew the victim and certainly could shed no light on the man's premature demise. But the two detectives weren't interested. We could do our talking, they said, at headquarters.

When we finally reached the station house, Clancy and I were just about at our wits' end. Explanation to the two officers had been futile. Now here we were in the middle of the night, being ushered into police headquarters. What a scene.

Up the staircase we marched to the top of the stairs where Chief of Detectives Nemo had his office. And there, cooling his heels outside of the office sat our friend Charlie Conacher, coach of the Chicago Black Hawks, whose club was in town to play the Leafs. The sight of Conacher set both Clancy and me back on our heels.

"Oh, my gosh, Charlie," I said, "you, too!"

Conacher was staring at the floor and never looked up. He just nodded his head.

Now Clancy and I were thinking about headlines that would say, "TWO NHL REFS AND COACH IMPLICATED IN MURDER."

Soon the door swung open and a dour Toronto policeman beckoned Clancy and Chadwick into the office. Behind a large desk sat Chief of Detectives Nemo, looking stern. I don't know about Clancy, but I don't mind saying that by now, I was pretty shaky.

"Sit down, gentlemen," said Detective Nemo, looking like Sherlock Holmes.

Clancy and I dropped into a couple of chairs.

"Did you see the morning papers about the murder?"

"Yes, sir, we did," I answered, "but we knew the man only casually."

"Almost not at all," interrupted Clancy, the color still drained from his face.

"Well, you know we found your names on him," the detective continued.

"Yes, but. . . ." Clancy never got his explanation out. He was interrupted by muffled laughter from outside the detective's office. The laugh belonged unmistakably to Conacher.

"Hey, what's going on here?" demanded Clancy, his face returning to its natural color for the first time since the affair began.

Into the room burst Conacher, absolutely doubled over in laughter. Detective Nemo smiled. Clancy and Chadwick had been taken. Conacher had put one over on us. He was a friend of the detectives, and knowing that we were acquaintances of the dead man, the Chicago coach had set us up for the hoax.

"I got you . . . I got you both," he said, gloating and half-hysterical. "All those lousy calls you've made all year—I got even for every one of them. Ha, ha, ha."

Conacher was laughing so hard, he almost had tears in his eyes. And after what Clancy said next, those tears could have been from something other than hysteria.

"You got us good," chuckled Clancy, a touch of benevolence creasing his face. "But wait until tomorrow night when you play the Leafs and one of us is refereeing. Then we'll see who gets whom."

9

SQUID ON ICE

The guy who kayoed me with the rolled up newspaper scored one of the very few knockouts I suffered in my career as an NHL official. So you'd have to credit him with one of the most effective anti-ref devices, but certainly not the most imaginative. No, sir. That honor has to go to an anonymous gallery god in that mecca of hockey gentility, Chicago Stadium.

I had some of my best adventures in Chicago. In addition to the Windy City incidents already described there was the time—probably the most frightening postgame experience of my career—when a disgruntled fan chased after the cab that was driving me to the railroad station. It was like a cops-and-robbers chase that you might see in the movies. It was positively scary and it didn't end until my cabbie shook the pursuing car with a two-wheel turn a block or two before the station. I was never so glad to get out of a town in all my life.

Now, of course, the routine things that get thrown at referees are the things most easily accessible to the fans. That would be beer, soda, peanuts, popcorn, and the other stuff fans can buy at the stadium. I have taken my share of beer baths, believe me. Then there is the more esoteric material. Once, I had false teeth thrown at me. Greater love for his team has no fan than the one who'll chew his food with his gums after tossing his choppers at the guy in the striped shirt. That's loyalty!

Another time—I think it was in Boston—a fan scored a direct hit on the top of my noggin with a string of firecrackers. When they started going off, I thought I had been shot. You don't know what to think. I reached up, expecting to find blood. Luckily, all there was on top of my head was some smoke.

Once, in Montreal, a fan threw a whiskey shot glass filled with some kind of liquid—I believe it was water—which landed at my foot and spilled. Butch Bouchard, the great Hall of Fame defenseman whose son now plays in the NHL, looked at the tiny puddle, then grinned at me. "Eh, Beel," he said in his thick French accent. "Somebodee throw you a cup of joy."

In Detroit I was working a Stanley Cup game when a package went sailing by. It barely missed me. I skated over to pick it up. When I bent over, I got one hell of a surprise. The damn thing was moving.

"What the hell? . . ." I shouted and wheeled off in the other direction. I thought it an octopus, but I later found out that it was a squid. The Detroit fans still use them to criticize officials. Squids. Alive. On the ice.

But the best of all—the absolute best—had to be in Chicago Stadium. My friend King Clancy had his problems in the same town with a lady fan who sat at rinkside for every game.

"Oh, she was a lovely lady," King often said. "Everytime I would jump onto the sideboards to get out of the way, she'd come running and jab me with a hatpin." Lovely lady.

One year I was working a Toronto-Black Hawk game in Chicago with my buddy, Sammy Babcock, as linesman. It wasn't the most exciting game I'd ever seen but it became one of the most memorable about halfway through the second period when somebody upstairs tossed a cardboard box on the ice.

Now long experience had taught me never to look into an unopened box that was thrown at me. You just never know what could jump out at you. On this particular occasion what jumped out was a floppy-eared rabbit.

I have seen a lot of strange sights in hockey rinks in my time, but that has to rate as the strangest. The poor little guy must have been frightened silly with 20,000 fans and a dozen or so hockey players howling at him. So he did what any self-respecting frightened bunny would do. He started hopping.

Now, in case you've never tried to catch a hopping rabbit on a hockey rink, I'm here to tell you it's no easy job. Especially when you're doubled over in laughter at the sight of the little guy scampering all over the ice.

Once, in the middle of the chase, Babcock skated by me and shouted, "Hey, Bill, Easter's not till April. What's this guy doing here now?"

The Leafs had two of the funniest guys in hockey at that time in goalie Turk Broda and defenseman Babe Pratt. Broda was a rotund individual who always had weight problems, and Pratt was a good-sized guy, too. Well, Pratt and Broda joined the chase, and it was beginning to look like a Keystone Kops comedy. Once, the rabbit scooted right under Pratt's legs and Babcock giggled. "Get your stick on the ice, Babe," he yelled. Pratt turned old floppy ears towards the net and Broda was set to field it. Naturally, the little guy skidded right past the goalie and into the net.

The goal judge squeezed his trigger, and the red light behind Broda's net went on, making everybody a little more hysterical.

"You shouda had it, Turk," criticized Pratt.

"Pucks I can stop," answered Broda. "With rabbits I'm not so good."

The rabbit knew Broda's net wasn't the safest spot in the

house either, so he scooted out of there in a hurry, and the merry chase continued. Next, he hippity-hopped his way to the Chicago penalty box and skipped in there.

"What'd you get him for, Bill?" asked one of the players.

I never broke stride. "Illegal equipment," I said. "He doesn't have skates."

Finally Babcock corralled the rabbit and carted him over to the timekeeper's bench where linesmen always bring broken sticks and other debris from the ice. The timekeeper, though, wasn't particularly anxious to accept this bit of debris.

"I don't want him," the man told Babcock. "What am I going to do with him?"

Well, by then, Babcock was pooped out—half from laughing and half from chasing that silly rabbit. And the one thing he wasn't in the mood for was backtalk from a minor official like a timekeeper. So he told the man off.

"I don't care what you do with him," said Sammy. "Hey, I've got an idea. Why don't you let him run the clock? He ought to be able to do that as well as you."

Babcock was very much like Clancy. He had a funny streak in him, a sense of humor that made it a pleasure to be around him. And, believe me, with some of the comedians we dealt with, you had to have a sense of humor.

There were some funny characters skating around the National Hockey League in those days. One of my favorites was Elmer Lach, the great center of the Montreal Canadiens.

Lach played center for Rocket Richard and Toe Blake. Together they formed one of the most powerful lines in NHL history. Elmer was a marvelous pivot and his tongue was every bit as good as his shot. He always had something to say, whether it was important or not.

I was in Montreal to start a season and the Canadiens were opening the game with the Lach line up front and Kenny Reardon on defense with Butch Bouchard. Reardon had married the daughter of Senator Donat Raymond the previous summer. That is a very secure position for a hockey player—being married to the boss's daughter. What's more, the Canadiens were only a minor part of Senator Donat's vast holdings.

As Lach leaned in for the face-off, he looked up at me. "Hey Bill," he said. "Did you hear, Kenny is going to school now?" nodding at Reardon.

Naturally, I was impressed. "No, Elmer," I said. "I didn't know that. What's he studying?"

"Oh, he's not going to school to learn how to make it anymore," said Lach, a smile curling his lips. "He's going to learn how to spend it."

One of Lach's teammates with Montreal was Murph Chamberlain, another excellent speechmaker. Chamberlain was a rough, tough hockey player who didn't care for anything or anybody. He wasn't bad in the elbow-bending department after games either. Murph played for Toronto, Boston, and New York Americans—where he fit right in with Red Dutton's zany cast of characters—and the Montreal Canadiens.

One of my "fondest" memories of Chamberlain was in the 1942–1943 season. That was my second year in the league and I decided to take my bride, Millie, on a trip to Boston with me. We stopped at the Manger Hotel, which was the regular home for hockey players and officials staying in Boston. The hotel, later renamed the Madison, is right next to North Station and a one-block walk to Boston Garden, where the Bruins play their games. So, because it was so convenient, it always attracted a hockey crowd.

On this particular night the management of the Manger Hotel made the mistake of billeting Mr. and Mrs. Bill Chadwick in a room right next door to one occupied by four hockey players. The four players were Yank Boyd, Buzz Boll, Harvey Jackson, and Mr. Chamberlain, and they decided to enliven an otherwise dull evening by hosting a party. That was very nice for them, but not so nice for the referee and his wife who were in the room next door.

Needless to say, the party got a little raucous but I don't think I would have minded it so much except for one thing. Chamberlain decided to evaluate the refereeing staff of the league and the terms he used for Chadwick weren't very nice. Millie still winces today when she thinks about that road trip and Murph Chamberlain's party.

A year after the party, Murph turned up in Montreal. That was understandable since we were in the midst of World War II and many hockey players, who weren't anxious to go off into the service, were shipped to teams in Canada. A whole load of players were shuttled out of the States because of the draft and Murph was one of them. The Canadiens put Chamberlain on a line with Phil Watson, who had been shipped to them from the New York Rangers, and Ray Getliffe. They were quite a line.

Getliffe threw his body around and later became a referee. I think he would have become a good one, too, except that he went into a more lucrative business. Watson was a wonderful conversationalist, especially in French, his native language. He was absolutely thrilled when he learned English because that meant he could give it to the referee in two languages instead of one. Chamberlain had a little streak of meanness in him, too. He would hurt you if he possibly could. You need that kind of a player on the hockey club.

The New York Rangers had one like that, or at least they liked to think they did, in a defenseman named Lou Fontinato. Now in those days, the Rangers didn't have much to talk about. They were a pretty awful hockey club. So, when Fontinato came along, they built him up into the rugged guy who would give them the kind of hitting New York fans have always thought was the first element for winning hockey.

The publicity buildup included a nickname for Fontinato. He would be known as Leaping Louie. That had a very nice sound to it, but I decided that Mr. Fontinato had better not try to live up to it in any game I refereed.

Early in his NHL career, Louie was playing in a game I was working. He began sounding off a little more than I cared for and I knew that we were heading for a confrontation. When it came, I was ready. Leaping Louie leaped, and before he came back down to the ice, he had himself a misconduct penalty. And do you know something? That was the only time Leaping Louie ever leaped in a game I refereed.

The Rangers' coach in those days was Muzz Patrick, my old teammate from the New York Rovers. Muzz made himself a hockey player. He was from a great hockey family. His father, Lester, and his uncle, Frank, were two of the game's first important builders and Muzz must have felt a responsibility to succeed at the sport. So he did. He also enjoyed success at several others as well. He was Canadian amateur cycle champion and heavyweight boxing champion. He also played on a championship basketball team in Canada.

Muzz was a friendly sort of a guy, big and gregarious. He made me feel at home with the Rovers, and that wasn't easy, surrounded by all the Canadian players. It was Muzz who marked my inauguration into the Rovers by throwing my nice new hat under a streetcar in Baltimore and laughing like hell at the mangled mess that emerged. It wasn't an act of anger but one of fun. And Muzz and I had our share of that commodity.

When he coached the Rangers, we had a ball all of the time. I'd skate by the bench with New York getting beaten and stop near Muzz. "Hey, Bill," he'd whisper. "How about a beer after the game?"

I'd say, "Sure, meet me at such-and-such-a-place."

It was strictly social. We were two ex-teammates and two good friends. As a coach he didn't have anybody to have a beer with, and as a referee I didn't have anybody to have a beer with. So we kept each other company, bending an elbow or two. And, I must say, Muzz was a pretty tough guy to keep up with in that department.

One of the reasons the Rangers had their troubles during those years were some trades that backfired. And none backfired quite so badly as the uneven swap they worked out with Toronto during the 1942-1943 season. New York got Hank Goldup, a nondescript forward who barely averaged ten goals a season in the six years he spent in the NHL. In exchange, the Maple Leafs received my friend Babe Pratt, a big defenseman who was a good enough hockey player to wind up in the Hall of Fame. Off the ice, though, Babe was a bit of a flake. In fact, come to think of it, he was sometimes flaky on the ice, too.

It was Pratt's Stanley Cup winning goal that got me in hot water with the Detroit organization after I had tagged Syd Howe with a penalty late in the seventh game of the playoffs. I heard it from the Red Wing bench when that happened, but if I hadn't called the penalty, I probably would have heard it from Pratt—not in the kind of terms that might have angered me, though. Babe wasn't that sort. He was more comical than cynical about everything that went on in the game. He'd never say enough so that you could hit him with anything. And when he spoke to you, you had to hold back to keep from breaking out in laughter. He was that funny.

Babe's son, Tracy, followed in his dad's footsteps and also made it to the NHL as a defenseman. Pratt often tells stories about Tracy's contract negotiations with people like Tommy Ivan of Chicago and Punch Imlach of Buffalo, and knowing those guys, I'd say Babe's tales of Tracy's woes are only slightly exaggerated.

Pratt stayed in the NHL when the league expanded and serves as a vice president of the Vancouver Canucks, who, ironically, traded for Tracy during the 1973 season. Pratt's main job with Vancouver is that of a goodwill ambassador who goes around making speeches. He's perfect for that function. He made plenty of speeches on the ice when he was playing.

Chicago had a pretty good public speaker, too, in Johnny Mariucci, the solitaire player. He was a product of Eveleth, Minnesota, the same town that sent goalies Mike Karakas and Frank Brimsek to the NHL. John went to the University of Minnesota, where he played end and was a good football player.

Mariucci tried to establish himself as a rough, tough hockey player, and I guess he was that. The only thing about him, though, was that he bounced up off the canvas too often. I think possibly he got a little punchy because the times I saw him fight he received more than he got.

John served in the coast guard during the war years and after that returned to the Black Hawks to finish out his playing career. When the NHL expanded, Mariucci was hired by Minnesota as an assistant to General Manager Wren Blair. He does scouting and other front office chores for the North Stars.

During my years in the NHL, there was a journeyman forward named Vic Lynn bouncing from team to team. He did time with five of the six clubs in the league and missed only the New York Rangers. That might, in retrospect, be a compliment to the Rangers. Lynn wasn't the most talented player of his era, and in his best season he scored only 14 goals for Boston. But I remember one game in which light-scoring Vic Lynn had two goals. And maybe, in my small way, I was responsible for his momentary success.

Lynn was playing for Toronto at that time, and early in the first period of this particular game he got his stick up a little high and I caught him. I raised my arm and whistled the penalty. Pointing at him, I shouted: "Lynn, I want you. Two minutes for a high stick."

Right away, Lynn started giving me a song-and-dance about how his stick wasn't up that high and how could I call a penalty like that and why didn't I call the other guy's hold against him and this and that until I'd really had an earful. Finally, I whirled on him.

"Look, you clown, you're not out here to referee," I said. "I'll take care of that job. Your job is to score goals for your team. Try doing that instead of yapping so much."

Lynn must have sensed that I was running out of patience with him because he retreated to the penalty box to serve his time. Later, he returned to score not one but two goals. The sight of Lynn scoring two goals in a single game was a shocker to everyone in the building. He usually couldn't get two in a week and sometimes in a month.

After his second goal Lynn glided past me with a big grin creasing his face. He stopped for a moment, looked over his shoulder, and winked. "Thanks, coach," he laughed.

10

SUDDEN DEATH

There is nothing quite like the pressure of the Stanley Cup, not only on the players but on the officials as well. You work a whole season toward this climax, and when it comes, you try your damnedest to perform up to the standards the playoffs deserve. I refereed 105 Stanley Cup games in my career and it is one of my proudest accomplishments; no NHL referee in history comes close to that total.

When you get down to the short strokes of a hockey season, every penalty becomes memorable. Especially when a call can turn an entire playoff series around. That's what happened to me during the 1946–1947 championship round between Toronto and Montreal.

The Canadiens were a powerhouse team. They finished first during the regular season for the fourth consecutive time and four of the six players selected to the official NHL All-Star team were from Montreal. They were goalie Bill Durnan, defensemen Butch Bouchard and Kenny Reardon, and right-winger Maurice Richard.

Durnan had won the Vezina Trophy as the league's leading goalie for the fourth straight year, and Richard, who scored 45 goals, was the league's Most Valuable Player. Those two, along with Reardon and Bouchard, headed an awesome Montreal cast. The Canadiens were clearly the class of the league and zoomed past Boston in the opening round of the playoffs, eliminating the Bruins in five games.

Meanwhile, second-place Toronto knocked off Detroit, also in five games, to set up an all-Canada playoff for the Cup. The Maple Leafs also had a pretty fair hockey club with players like Turk Broda, Syl Apps, Bill Ezinicki, Teeder Kennedy, and Howie Meeker, who had been voted Rookie of the Year.

Meeker was an inspiration to the Leafs. He had been so badly wounded during the war that he was told he'd never play hockey again. But army doctors can't always measure the size of a man's heart or the amount of desire he has inside him. So, a year after the war ended, Howie Meeker, war wound and all, was the best damn rookie in the whole NHL. Maybe it was that kind of determination that helped the Maple Leafs in their seemingly one-sided championship series against Montreal.

The Canadiens won the first game of the final round, 6-0, and they did it so easily that they hardly seemed to work up a sweat. Toronto, it seemed, just had no business being on the same ice with the Canadiens. And Bill Durnan decided to needle the Leafs afterward.

"How did those guys get into the playoffs?" scoffed Durnan.

He soon found out. It is an old adage in sports that you let sleeping dogs lie. Durnan's crack helped wake up the Maple Leafs.

In game two of the series Toronto assigned pesky Vic Lynn to check Rocket Richard. Lynn was nothing more than an agitator, and Richard's low boiling point got the better of the Rocket. After one or two wrestling matches, Richard gave Lynn a high stick and cut him on the head. I saw the play and never hesitated. It was five minutes in the penalty box for Richard for cutting the Toronto player.

I'll say this for Richard, who never was one of my favorite players. If I had a stick in my hands, I'd have high-sticked Vic Lynn, too, because he wasn't a very likable hockey player and made a career of aggravating Richard terribly.

Now Rocket Richard wasn't the most forgiving individual in the NHL, and you could almost see the steam escaping from his ears as he sat in the penalty box. I knew when I looked over there that both the Maple Leafs and Bill Chadwick hadn't seen or heard the last of Richard that night.

We got into the second period of the game and Richard was back on the ice. Sure enough, he got tangled up, this time with Bill Ezinicki. Now no one ever had to worry about Ezinicki. He was a tough hockey player who knew how to take care of himself. Some people labeled him a dirty hockey player because he led the league in penalties a couple of years. But I never thought of him that way. He just went all out and hit with his body—sometimes legally, sometimes not so legally.

I got between Richard and Ezinicki and just as I did, I got a look at Richard's eyes. I've never seen a man that angry. Just as I got between them, Richard reached over my shoulder with both hands on his stick and pole-axed Ezinicki right in the middle of the head.

Ezinicki went down in a heap, and if they hadn't pulled Richard away, I think he would have torn Ezzy apart while he was stretched out there on the ice. Rocket had given me no choice. It was clearly a match penalty for deliberate attempt to injure an opponent.

That kind of penalty today leaves the offending player's team shorthanded for five minutes. But in those days, it was 20 minutes shorthanded. Even the powerful Canadiens couldn't skate shorthanded that long without getting hurt. Toronto scored a couple of goals during that period-long power play and shut out Montreal, 4-0. That evened the playoff at one victory apiece and sent the two teams to Toronto for game three. Richard, however, didn't go along.

Clarence Campbell, completing his first year as president of the league, decided to step into the second-game mess. He tagged Richard with an additional $250 fine and suspended him for one game.

Now you must understand that Maurice Richard at that time could have been elected prime minister of Canada. He was that popular a hockey player, especially with the French fans. Suspending him was a brave thing for Campbell to do, especially in the midst of the championship playoff. It was entirely proper if you ask me, but not if you ask Montreal fans. When Toronto took the game that Richard had to sit out and the next one as well for a 3–1 lead in the best-of-seven series, the anger of the fans just increased.

Montreal won the fifth game, but the Canadiens were staggering and just unable to stem the Leafs' surge. Toronto took game six and the Cup, the first of three straight Stanley Cups for the Maple Leafs.

Canadien fans blamed the defeat on the Richard incident, although strangely all of the criticism was heaped on Campbell and none of it on Chadwick. To this day, Campbell, even though he is a longtime resident of the city, is not a favorite in Montreal. But the people of the town never took it out on me.

Three years earlier, in 1944, in another Montreal-Toronto playoff, Richard had emerged in a much different role. He quite simply put on the greatest single-man performance I have ever seen in playoff competition. The Canadiens had lost the first game of the semifinal series to Toronto, 3–1, and for game two big Bob Davidson was back on the job, shadowing the Rocket. That was Davidson's job. He played on a line with Syl Apps and Bill Ezinicki, and his total of 94 goals in 12 big league seasons with the Leafs is eloquent testimony to the fact that Davidson was on the ice not because he was a scoring threat but because he was a tenacious checker.

Richard was only in his second NHL season but already was considered enough of a scoring threat to warrant special checking attention. And when the Canadiens played the Leafs, Davidson was the man charged with watching the Rocket. That was his primary objective—to hold Richard in check. Most of the time he did the job well, and in my opinion, he was one of the best defensive forwards around. And he usually did the job without incurring many penalties. He was just a solid checker, and he did possibly the best job of checking that anybody could on one of the most prolific scorers in NHL history. On this night, though, nobody, not even Bob Davidson, could keep up with Richard.

In the first period Davidson and the Leafs kept Richard off the score sheet, and it was a 0-0 hockey game. That meant that in four periods on their home ice Montreal had managed only one goal against Toronto. The Canadiens were clearly due to break out, and in the next two periods Rocket Richard did just that.

Less than two minutes into the second period Richard took passes from Toe Blake and Mike McMahon and zoomed in to beat Toronto goalie Paul Bibeault for the game's first goal. Seventeen seconds later Richard was back on Bibeault's doorstep again, this time converting passes from his linemates, Blake, Elmer, and Lach.

When the Canadiens surged two goals ahead, it forced the Maple Leafs to open the game up a bit. Toronto had to get some goals of its own, and Reg Hamilton provided one at 8:50 of the period, narrowing the Montreal lead to 2-1. But eight minutes later Richard connected again for his third goal of the game—a Stanley Cup hat trick—three goals not in one game but in one period!

By then Richard had the French fans in a frenzy, roaring

at his every move. In the third period Lach and Blake fed him for the third time in the game and he scored his fourth goal after only one minute of play. Then, at 8:34, he scored number five. The final score of the game was Richard 5, Toronto 1.

It is traditional at hockey games to have a writer or broadcaster select the game's three stars after the final buzzer. Usually, they are announced with the number three star first, then number two, and finally number one, so the crowd can build up a crescendo of applause. As I was leaving the ice, the announcer began.

"Tonight's third star," said the public address man, "number 9, Maurice Richard."

A dumbfounded silence fell over the crowd in the Montreal Forum. How could that be? How could a man score all five of his team's goals and be named third star.

In the dressing room runway the announcement even stopped me in my tracks. "Is that guy kidding?" I said.

Now the announcer continued. "Tonight's second star," he said, "number 9, Maurice Richard."

With that, the crowd began to understand. Richard wasn't being shrugged off with a third-star designation on his big night. Instead, he was being saluted in a way no other hockey player has ever been saluted. A roar began to spill down from the upper reaches of the Forum and soon it encompassed the whole building.

"And tonight's first star," the announcer continued, "number 9, Maurice Richard."

In the dressing room Richard mused about his feat. "I only had six or seven shots on net all game," he said, "and each goal was scored in a different way. The Leafs are a close checking club and they always put Davidson out to check me every game. Sometimes he stays so close to me that I get angry. Tonight, I guess, I took it out on him and the puck."

The ironic thing about it is that three games later,

Montreal really belted the Leafs, 11-0, and the Rocket only had two goals in that game.

One of the things that makes playoff hockey extra special is the overtime element. During the regular season, if the game is tied at the end of the three periods, both teams take one point and go home. But when the Cup is on the line, every game is played to a conclusion—no matter how long it takes.

Overtime adds an extra dimension of sudden death to the games, and if you think playoff hockey is exciting, you can't believe the tension of those games when they stretch into extra periods. If you could stand the excitement of sudden death, then the best playoff year the NHL ever had was 1951, when eight games were decided by overtimes.

It started in the very first Cup game that spring with Montreal playing at Detroit. The game was tied at 2-2 when regulation time ran out. After a brief intermission to resurface the ice, the teams went back at it.

The first overtime was scoreless. Then, in the second, Montreal buzzed around the Detroit net. Terry Sawchuk was the Red Wing goalie, and he was sprawling all over the place, holding off the Canadiens. Suddenly, the puck came to Rocket Richard, and in an instant the red goal light behind Sawchuk went on. The Montreal players thrust their sticks in the air in triumph. I guess they didn't see me waving the goal off until a few seconds later.

Richard, as might be expected, yelled loudest and said his usual quota of uncomplimentary things. But it was no goal, and that was that. Richard had kicked the goal in and you're not allowed to score that way.

It took several minutes to calm the Canadiens down but eventually play resumed. Next it was Detroit's turn to get mad. Some time elapsed and soon the Red Wings were testing Gerry McNeil in the Montreal nets. Suddenly, the puck was behind McNeil and the Detroit players were hugging each other in celebration. But there at the side of the net was Chadwick, waving his arms and shaking his head. "No goal!" I shouted.

Now the Red Wings rushed me. It was like an instant replay. Only the color of the jerseys was different. A few minutes before, the Canadiens had been giving it to me. Now it was Detroit's turn. The funny thing about it was that the reason I disallowed the goal was very similar to the reason I had ruled Richard's shot no goal. This time Glen Skov had directed the puck into the net with his skate, and that's a no-no. If the puck had deflected in off Skov's skate, it would have been okay. But Glen was tied up in front of McNeil and had used his foot to turn the puck past the goalie.

When we got to the dressing room after the third overtime period, I wondered to myself whether the thing would ever end. It was beginning to look like we'd be there forever. But 69 seconds into the fourth overtime Richard broke in on Sawchuk and beat him cleanly for the deciding goal. As the Canadiens swarmed around the Rocket, one of them skated past me. In a tone just loud enough for me to hear, he said, "Thank God nobody kicked that one in." To which I added a silent "Amen."

The game was in its seventh period when Richard ended it after 121 minutes of hockey. It was 1:00 A.M. when it ended, and it is the longest game I ever handled. My ankles were still swollen the next morning.

Two nights later, in the second game of their series, the Canadiens and Red Wings went at it again. This time the game was scoreless after regulation time had expired and the teams then struggled through two more overtimes without a goal being scored.

Finally, Rocket Richard settled the issue again with a goal at 2:20 of the third overtime. That meant the teams had played a total of 11 full periods of hockey in the first two games of their playoff series.

You would think two heartbreaking overtime losses like that would just kill a hockey club. But the Red Wings didn't die easily. They came right back to beat the Canadiens two straight in Montreal, tying the playoff. But then Richard and company won the next two games to advance to the playoff finals.

In the other series, Toronto eliminated Boston, four victories to one. Another game in the playoff ended in a 1–1 tie and was halted after one overtime only because of a Saturday night curfew law in Toronto.

That set up a showdown for the Cup between the Canadiens and Maple Leafs. It has to rank as one of the most memorable Stanley Cup series in history. It lasted five games and every one of those five games went into sudden-death overtime.

The first game was at Toronto, and with the score tied at 2–2 near the end of regulation time, Richard zoomed in on an unprotected Maple Leaf net. As he fired, Bill Barilko, a Toronto defenseman, dove full length to block the shot and preserve the tie. That turned out to be a game-saving play, because Sid Smith's goal six minutes into the first overtime gave the Leafs the victory.

Richard got the Canadiens even in game two, scoring the winning overtime goal in a 3–2 Montreal victory. That was one of the five times in his career that the Rocket settled an overtime Stanley Cup game.

The series moved to Montreal and the Leafs stunned the Canadiens by winning the next two games in the Forum, both in overtime. Teeder Kennedy's goal won game three, and Harry Watson's gave Toronto the victory in game four.

Now it was back to Toronto for the fifth game, and this time it didn't look like the game would go beyond the regulation 60 minutes of playing time. Montreal was leading, 2–1, in the final minute when Toronto coach Joe Primeau lifted his goalie for an extra attacker. And there, with the empty Leaf goal gaping at them, the Canadiens couldn't get the clincher. Instead, Toronto came down the ice and set up shop in the Canadiens' zone. They worked the puck to Tod Sloan, and with 32 seconds left on the clock he scored, tying the game at

2-2 and forcing a fifth straight overtime between the two teams.

Early in the extra period the issue was settled. Bill Barilko, a quiet guy who never was much of scorer but played a steady kind of defense, was skating at mid-ice when Howie Meeker slipped the puck to him. As he moved over the blue line, he whipped a desperation shot at McNeil. Barilko went hurtling into the air just as the puck hit the net. The game was over. The Maple Leafs were champions.

That was the last goal Bill Barilko ever scored. That summer he and a friend, Dr. Henry Hudson, flew into northern Canada on a fishing trip in the doctor's private plane. They were never heard from again.

11
MY TEAM

In my career as an NHL official—two years as a linesman, and then 14 more as a referee—I had the privilege of
watching some of the greatest players ever to lace on a pair of
skates. Many of them have been honored with eventual induction into hockey's Hall of Fame, an honor they richly deserved
for their performances on the ice.

It isn't easy to separate these guys and say which ones
were the best at their positions. How could you decide between
Bill Durnan and Turk Broda in goal? Or Gordie Howe and
Rocket Richard on right wing? So when people ask me to
select my all-time all-star team, I never name just six players.
My squad numbers 11 players, and even though that's more
than you'd expect to find, I'm not going to reduce it. I'm the
referee in this game, and we're playing by my rules.

I've picked two goalies for my all-time team. They are Bill
Durnan of Montreal and Turk Broda of Toronto, and I'd split
the chores between them with Durnan doing most of the regular season work and Broda my playoff choice.

On defense I'll go with Detroit's Black Jack Stewart and
Dit Clapper, who played 20 years for Boston, on one team and

Red Kelly of Detroit with Montreal's Doug Harvey on another.

My centers are Milt Schmidt of Boston, probably the finest all-around player I've ever seen, and Montreal's Jean Beliveau. Detroit's Ted Lindsay, who wasn't my favorite individual, would have to be the left wing, and I'll go with Rocket Richard of Montreal and Gordie Howe of Detroit on right wing.

Let's take them one by one.

Schmidt was my favorite. A tremendous skater and a fabulous playmaker, Milt had more guts than any player in the league. He was and is a high-class guy.

In most of the years I refereed the Boston Bruins were just not in contention. They had a first-class hockey player in Schmidt but little talent to help him. Most of the time, Boston was out of the game in the first period. There was, I am told, a stretch of 22 straight games that I refereed which the Boston Bruins did not win. That fact did not make me the most popular visitor in the city of Boston.

But the inept play of the Bruins never tarnished the greatness of Schmidt. I was a tremendous admirer of the guy. He knew it and he respected me and I respected him. Many times something would happen on the ice, particularly in Boston Garden, and Schmidt, as captain of the Bruins, would skate over to me for a little discussion, just to liven up the game.

Milt would stand with his hands on his hips and shake his head from side to side. His mouth would be going like crazy, and he'd be saying, "Bill, how is your family?"

I'd stand there doing the same thing and answer, "Fine. How is yours, Milt?"

After a few minutes, he'd skate away in one direction and I'd go off in another while the Bruins fans went crazy. They thought he was giving me hell, which possibly sometimes he should have but didn't.

Often, Milt would be back-checking after a play would finish off in the Boston zone and I always refereed from center ice, not on the boards. I'd always follow the center up ice and Milt and I would have races. He'd be tired toward the end of his little stint on the ice, and of course, he could beat me any time he'd want. I'd never admit that then, only now. I'd say, "C'mon Milt, let's go. See who wins down to the other end of the ice." Then he'd go and I'd go. Of course I had a few other things to do besides getting down to the other end, and so he won most of our little races.

Schmidt was one tremendous competitor, and in Detroit the Red Wings had the same kind of guy on defense in Jack Stewart. He was very much like Schmidt, who came to play the game every night he was on the ice. And when Detroit and Boston were pitted against each other, Schmidt and Stewart put on a show.

It was like a personal vendetta between them with each trying to outdo the other. Their collisions were something. Ten other forwards and defensemen on the ice would be concerned with Detroit versus Boston. But for those two, it was strictly Schmidt versus Stewart. They'd come in contact with each other at every opportunity and see who could best the other. It was a great contest and there wasn't any dirty stuff with either one of them.

They very seldom got penalties against each other. Milt would come down the ice, glide over the blue line, and when he'd see Stewart, he'd just jump and plow into him. And Stewart would try to knock him down. It was a contest every game and it was great to be part of that era because they played all the way.

Dit Clapper was the same kind of defenseman as Stewart. He'd stand up there at the blue line and challenge a forward to get past him. And I can tell you that not too many of those forwards took up or won that challenge.

Stewart and Clapper played in the era when the red line

was being introduced to the National Hockey League. It was a different style of hockey from the modern racehorse game. And for that later era, my defensemen would be Red Kelly and Doug Harvey.

Kelly was a tremendous puck handler, and his ability showed when he was traded from Detroit to Toronto and converted into an all-star center. In my opinion, there has never been a better playmaker among defensemen than Harvey, who was the heart of Montreal's great teams during the 1950s.

Those two started the turnaround of styles for defensemen. We always hear how the guy who introduced the rushing game for defensemen into hockey was Bobby Orr. Well, that's a lot of bull. Harvey and Kelly were carrying the puck out of their zones and setting up plays when Orr was still in grade school. Orr gets all the credit for the development of the offensive-minded defenseman. The guys who started it were Kelly and Harvey. They were the ones who moved the puck. Neither one of them could skate or shoot like a Bobby Orr, but they started this style of hockey.

Harvey was a genius, especially on the power play. He'd direct that Montreal attack like a quarterback, sitting out there at the blue line, throwing the puck to the open man. Often, the Canadiens would score two and three goals on a single power play because they got so proficient at converting that manpower advantage. And the man who was the key to that success was Harvey. Eventually, as already mentioned, the NHL had to change the rules and allow a penalized player to return to the ice as soon as his team gave up a goal instead of sitting out the full term of his penalty. The reason that change was made was because of the Montreal Canadiens.

In 1952 the Canadiens came up with a pretty good center by the name of Jean Beliveau. Beliveau had been playing in the American Hockey League with Quebec City and, I understand, was making as much or more money there as he could with the Canadiens in the NHL. So Beliveau wasn't too anxious to move up to the NHL. But when he did, there was no mistaking the man's enormous talent.

When the Canadiens called him up, it was for a three-game trial. That was common practice for new players in those days. I was the referee in the first game Beliveau played in the NHL, and I remember wondering before the game just how good this highly heralded young center would be. Well, let me tell you, it didn't take long to realize that Beliveau's reputation was not inflated. He got a couple of goals and an assist and you knew, just watching him in that first game, that he had class and was a shade above the other players.

Beliveau had finesse. He was a marvelous skater and a superb stickhandler. I remember after leaving the ice in that first game he played saying to myself that Mr. Beliveau was going to be a great one. Time has proven that rather hasty analysis to be accurate.

In the years that I refereed, the two greatest scoring wings were Ted Lindsay and Rocket Richard. They were both tremendous hockey players who would do anything that needed to be done in order to score a goal. Both of them made my life tough, but that can not diminish the respect I feel for the skills of both when it comes to playing this game.

Lindsay was the best left wing I ever saw. If I were a coach, he's the kind of guy I'd love to have playing for me. A lot of people call him a dirty hockey player, and it's true that he spent more time in penalty boxes than anybody else in the history of the NHL. He would do anything to score a goal, even if it meant going as far as chopping somebody's head off. If playing dirty meant he could score a goal, well then, he'd play dirty. He was doing what he thought was right for the Detroit Red Wings. Whether or not it hurt Bill Chadwick had no bearing on it.

Lindsay was simply a mean hockey player. He would do anything to anybody standing in his way. I once saw him knock out Jerry Toppazzini and then continue to pummel away at the guy even after he was flat on the ice. That's mean. Of course, he was penalized for his action.

Lindsay was just a nasty individual on the ice but he made it pay off for him. There was a showdown between him and me every year. As soon as I refereed the first game of the year in which he was playing, I had to get the upper hand. I had to prove to him I was boss and if I didn't do it in the very beginning of the season, then I was gone the rest of the year. So I'd go out there looking to nail Lindsay for a rule infraction just as fast as I could. It got to a point where it was a battle between Chadwick and Lindsay. He wasn't going to get away with a thing as far as I was concerned.

I was a fair referee and I never called a penalty without reason. But I'll tell you this: With guys like Lindsay and Rocket Richard (who was cut from the same mold) I made sure I called the first penalty I could. With those two guys, I broke my own rule of ignoring remarks that weren't heard by somebody else. As soon as they opened their mouths or stepped over the line, they were gone. The reason for that was I knew I'd be hearing from them the rest of the year, and if I tried to call one on them later that hadn't been called earlier, they'd bitch, and probably rightfully, about why I hadn't gotten them for it the first time it had happened two months before.

Richard was in a class by himself as a great hockey player, particularly in the playoffs when the money was on the line. Rocket had a nose for the goal, and from the blue line in he would explode. He played as if there were three red goal lights, two in the eyes of the goaltender and one in the back of the net.

If you needed a goal, the Rocket would get it for you. And he'd take somebody's eye out to do it. He didn't care what it took, as long as he put it in the net. Many times I saw the toughest defensemen in the NHL, guys like Jack Stewart and

Earl Siebert, riding Rocket's back, and still Richard would control the puck and get it by the goaltender.

Rocket was the same kind of an individual as Lindsay—perhaps more intense than Lindsay but not quite as smart. And Lindsay has proven that in later years with business successes in Detroit while Rocket has had his problems.

Rocket was a mean guy on and off the ice. He never had anything good to say about anybody. And he could never control himself. He was so emotional he would just go wild. His eyes would light up like the goal lights. He had a fire inside of him that I've seldom seen before or since.

If I just wanted to win hockey games, then Gordie Howe was the zenith in a hockey player because he could go both ways. But at the start of his career he was just another hockey player. I think he didn't have enough minor league experience and it took him a year or two to put it all together. But once he did, Howe became one of the game's real giants—a classic hockey player who could do everything well.

Bill Durnan was the finest goaltender I ever saw, but in the playoffs at least, Turk Broda was his equal. Durnan, of course, was ambidextrous. He'd come out there wearing conventional gloves on both hands and he could switch his stick from hand to hand, depending on which side of the ice the play was coming from.

Durnan also was a terrific puckhandler. He was one of the first to develop that ability, and although he couldn't handle it as well as, say, a Jacques Plante, he still helped himself a great deal with that special ability. Bill was also a very big man and he filled the nets. Of course, he had a great hockey club working in front of him in Montreal with guys like Butch Bouchard and Kenny Reardon on defense and forwards like Toe Blake, Elmer Lach, and Rocket Richard up front.

In the playoffs Broda always came up with the big game. And Turk didn't have the hockey clubs in front of him that Durnan did. Broda was a funny man who always had a quip to break the tension. He was a happy-go-lucky sort of an individual and I imagine that helped him as a goalie.

Broda was involved in one of the funniest playoff scenes I can remember. Here we were in the finals for the Stanley Cup, and everybody was tighter than a drum. The NHL had sent Chadwick and his old Rover linemate, Sammy Babcock, another pretty funny guy, to referee one game involving the Maple Leafs; Broda, of course was in the nets.

The Leafs were on the attack, pressuring the other team, when finally somebody iced the puck. It skidded past Broda into a corner and Babcock hurried to retrieve it. I was back there with Sammy but it was the linesman's job to pick up the puck or anything else that was on the ice. I always felt that it added something to my stature as the referee to leave those chores to my linesmen.

Well, anyway, Babcock bent over to get the puck and as he straightened up, he began to slip. His feet went out from under him and he went flat on his ass, right at Broda's feet. Turk looked at him with a perfectly straight face and said, "Geez, Sammy, you're gonna have a hell of a time seeing the offsides from there!"

That leaves a coach for this mythical team of mine. Probably the most successful coach of my era was Jack Adams, but he can't coach my team. We'd never get along. There was never any love lost between us. I felt that he and his boss, Old Man Norris, were trying to take the food out of my children's mouths. And they would have succeeded except for the fact that there were five others on the board of governors who were determined to shove me right down Detroit's throat.

Still, as a coach, Adams was one of the finest. But Hap Day of Toronto was every bit as good, and he'd be my man. Day was a very intelligent individual and a good handler of men. The same is true, really, of Montreal's Dick Irvin. Those three, Adams, Day, and Irvin, were all excellent coaches. Day and Irvin could work for my team. Adams would have to find employment elsewhere.

Now I know I'm going to get some flack on my team from a lot of people, especially my friends in the press box who hear from me when they pick the wrong stars of a game. They'll be asking, "What about the moderns—the Phil Espositos and Bobby Orrs?" Well, this team is my team from my era when I was a referee and they'll have to accept it on that basis. I've watched the Orrs and Espositos and I've got my share of opinions on those guys, too. I'll get to them later. But for now, drop the puck and I think the guys I've picked will do pretty well with it.

12
NUMBER 1

My wife, Millie, and my youngsters, Billy and Barbara, were proud that I was a referee in the National Hockey League. But it was never any fun for them to go to a hockey game. In the beginning my children were too young to understand what was happening. But Millie never liked to go and listen to the criticism that was heaped on me. She could never understand why or how fans could act the way they did.

To be a competent referee, you have to be able to stand separation from your family. Hockey players are home for half a season. I was home for one-sixth of the season. There was no such thing as being home for the holidays, and I must admit that I sometimes wondered if there was some kind of Scrooge sitting in the league office drawing up the schedules of the officials.

One year, at Christmas, the schedule had a game in New York and another game in Toronto. The league sent Norman Lamport, who lived in Toronto, to referee the game in New York and Bill Chadwick, who lived in New York, to referee the game in Toronto. Later, the same thing happened with George Gravel, who came from Montreal, and me. It would have been so easy for us both to be at home. But we weren't. I spent plenty of holidays in hotel lobbies and movie theaters.

It was quite a job for Millie, who had to live alone and for half a year, to bring up the children by herself. Every summer we made a special effort to make up my absences to the children. But you really never compensate for the time you lose. An athlete can only be as good as his family will allow him to be, and that goes for a referee or umpire, too. An awful lot of credit for any success I may have achieved has to go to Millie.

We always made April our big month. My mother's birthday was April 19. My son Billy was born on April 21 and Barbara's birthday is April 25, the day before our anniversary. Barbara was born in 1944 and she was always something of a tomboy. When she was 18 months old, I had a special pair of skates built for her by a guy in Chicago. She was an ice veteran by the time Billy came along in 1948. Those skates are still in our family and Barbara's children have used them.

With all those birthdays and our anniversary, April has always been a Christmas for us. It also marked the end of the long, long season and a chance, at last, to see my family again. Sometimes, Millie and our two blond youngsters would rush the reunion.

I'd be on the road going from city to city for maybe four or five weeks at a stretch, living out of my suitcase and getting a little tired of the whole thing. Then I'd pull into a city, and out of nowhere I'd find Millie and the kids waiting there for me. It was the greatest lift in the world.

One time, Millie took Billy and Barbara up to Boston for a playoff game without ever telling me. Into Boston Garden they walked, expecting to buy tickets with no problem. Well, playoff tickets aren't that easy to arrange, even when you have time to set them up. Getting them on the spur of the moment is next to impossible. But so is being the wife of a referee. As a result, it was no big deal for Mrs. Chadwick. Somehow, she talked her way into the building.

Well, the current fans in Boston Garden haven't changed one bit from those days. They have always been rough on the referee, and along about the third period they were giving it to me pretty good and Millie was suffering. All around her, Bruin fans were yelling for my scalp and I'm sure it was tearing her apart. Then Barbara Chadwick, age 9, took matters into her own hands.

One character seated behind my family began tearing into me with particular vengeance when Barbara turned around.

"Hey, you," said the referee's daughter. "You can't talk that way about the referee. He's my father."

That was the last my family heard from those particular Bruin fans that night. Thank you, Barbara.

There comes a time in every man's career in sports when he realizes that he must consider moving on. Eventually, time catches up with everyone. To be very honest, I hadn't given that development much thought until midway through the 1954-1955 season. There had been one brief overture from the Montreal organization asking if I'd be interested in the general manager's job with their Buffalo farm club in the American Hockey League. But the financial arrangements weren't satisfactory, so I stayed with the whistle.

Frankly, I had no thought of putting it away until one day midway through that 1954-1955 season when I received an offer to manage a new country club near my home on Long Island. The offer came from a syndicate that owned a beach club I had run for two or three summers. When the syndicate purchased the Consuelo Vanderbilt Balsam Estate in East Norwich, New York, to establish the Pine Hollow Country Club, they asked me if I would manage it.

I had never really managed anything before, but my refereeing career in the NHL gave me the confidence in myself, and I decided that I could do the job. There were other factors, too. I would see more of my family, I would be making more money, and perhaps most important, I decided that I couldn't go any further in refereeing. I was at the very top and I decided that this was the time to get out. So, at the age of thirty-nine and after sixteen NHL seasons, I decided to retire.

The league tried to get me to change my mind. Clarence Campbell called and offered me a blank check—really anything I wanted. If it was a matter of money, Campbell said, adjustments could be made. But that wasn't it at all. It was never my nature to argue salary. I have always felt that if you have to argue for something, then it takes the shine off getting it. It's the same as having to tell somebody how important you are. If you have to do that, well then, you're not very important.

The last game I refereed was the seventh game of the 1955 Stanley Cup finals. I felt that was a good way to go out and I've never had any reason to change my mind about that.

Over the years, people have asked me my philosophy of refereeing. I must admit it's a pretty tough thing to philosophize about being a ref. But I always felt, from the very beginning of my career, that learning the rule book was a minimal part of refereeing a hockey game. Refereeing must be accomplished by common sense. Knowing the rules and applying them are two entirely different things.

The players come to learn exactly what you're going to do—what you'll let them get away with and what you'll call them on. I used to skate alongside guys on marginal calls and tell them, "Don't do that again or I'll have to call it." I think that helped me gain a lot of respect. And respect is the key to an official's efficiency and success. If you can gain the respect of the top players, then you've got it made. It took me a couple of years to do that, but once it happened, my job became easier.

The thing about officiating is to set a standard and abide by it. What bugs me, then and now, is that often a referee will start the game one way and then change direction in mid-stream. Some refs will call everything right away and then let the game go. Or, probably even worse than that, is to let the game go at the start and then try to catch up to it later. No referee can possibly do that. You're better off letting them go all the way and kick one another's heads off than you are when you start to let them go and then try to put a lasso around them later.

I discovered a long time ago that nobody is going to pat you on the back and tell you what a wonderful job you're doing. Five years after I retired they put me in the Hall of Fame. That was the first time and, as a matter of fact, the only time they ever told me I was doing a good job. But over the second half of my career, referees began wearing numbers. They gave me number 1, and I always wore that number. I like to think it was significant.

13
YOU'RE ON THE AIR

The first year I was out of hockey, I missed the game very much. You don't just turn your back on sixteen years of your life without feeling something. But eventually, as I got deeply involved in the operation of the golf club, I became little more than a casual fan. I went to maybe six or eight games a season at Madison Square Garden and watched the game on television, but my deep involvement with sports was in our club. I just didn't have time to miss hockey.

In 1957 we ran the Pepsi-Cola Open with first-prize money of $9,000, which in 1957 wasn't all that bad. The tournament was won by a young golfer from Latrobe, Pennsylvania, who had never achieved first place in a "big money" tournament before. I understand Arnold Palmer has done pretty well since taking that one.

I stayed at Pine Hollow until 1960 and then moved on into another private industry. And I was perfectly content with what I was doing. I had left sports on top. I went out with a good name and I was content. Then, one day in 1968 a phone call came that changed my life around every bit as much as that telegram from Frank Calder had twenty-five years before.

The man on the other end of the line was Emile Francis, general manager of the New York Rangers. Francis is a dandy little front office administrator, and it's a good thing, because he'd never be remembered for his playing career. He was a journeyman goaltender who played parts of six NHL seasons with Chicago and New York, compiling a rather unsensational 3.74 goals-against average. He's a much better GM than that.

My most vivid memory of Francis as a player came in the last game of the 1947–1948 season when he was with the Black Hawks and playing in Madison Square Garden against the Rangers. New York's Buddy O'Connor was in a neck-and-neck race with Elmer Lach of Montreal for the scoring title, and the Rangers were determined to get O'Connor the title. They must have had him on the ice 40 minutes that night against Francis. And every time the Rangers got the puck, they looked to spring O'Connor. It was a weird show, but Francis held him off and Lach wound up with the scoring title by a single point.

After finishing his playing career, Francis moved into coaching in the Rangers' minor league system and then came to New York, first as assistant general manager and eventually as GM in 1964. That was when he began rebuilding the Rangers into a Stanley Cup contender, and a couple of years later his refurbishing included an old ex-referee.

In my phone conversation with Francis he asked me to stop by the Ranger offices. I told him I would and wondered what the Ranger boss had on his mind. I never could have guessed, and I must admit I was kind of surprised when he told me.

"Bill," he said, "we're looking for a man to hold between-periods interviews on our radio broadcasts. Are you interested?"

"I'm no broadcaster, Emile. Why me?" I asked.

"You've got a lot of friends in the game and you could

give our listeners good insight into the games," said Francis. "Why not give it a try?"

I must admit that Francis's offer flattered and excited me. It was a chance to get back into hockey, the game I loved so much and that was so much a part of my existence. It also offered a new challenge for me at a time in life when men don't often have an opportunity at new challenges. I think it was that more than anything else that induced me to accept Francis's offer.

The Ranger play-by-play man was a marvelously talented young man named Marv Albert, who had a super knack for keeping up with the radio description of the fastest game in the world. Albert would carry on a racehorse description of the game and I would sit there with my lip buttoned until it came time for the intermission, when I had maybe ten minutes of air time for my interview.

I must admit I wasn't comfortable in my situation. For one thing I felt muzzled during the action. There would be moments when I thought I could offer some helpful insight to go with Albert's description. For another, I wasn't a professional broadcaster and I suffered a certain amount of mike fright during those intermission interviews.

I solved both problems in short order. Marv and I talked with Francis and decided that my comments on the action during the game would help the program. For the interviews I developed a system of notes to myself during the conversations to keep them moving along comfortably. Slowly but surely, I was fitting in nicely as part of hockey's media, a part of the game I had never experienced before.

There was one aspect of it that I had gone through before, however. That was the problems of travel. I always prided myself on never missing an assignment in 16 years as an NHL official. There were some close calls, though. I haven't blown a broadcasting assignment yet either, but again, I've had some close ones.

My best travel adventure as a referee came during the 1947 season. I always made a practice of leaving a day early for assignments to be sure I'd be on time. This particular assignment was in Montreal and the Scrooge in the NHL schedule office struck again. On Christmas night I packed an overnight bag and headed for Grand Central Station for the trip north.

I was leaving on an 11:30 train and I got to the station in plenty of time. Outside a terrific snowstorm was in progress. It dumped about two feet of snow on the city. I headed for the club car, had a couple of beers, and went to bed.

The next morning I woke up at about ten o'clock, expecting to be called for customs at Rouses Point, the train's regular border crossing. Instead, I was in Harmon, New York, about 35 miles from Manhattan, where they swtiched from electric to steam engines. I was rather red in the neck, and frankly I didn't know what the hell to do.

Eventually, they coupled on the steam locomotive and we started huffing and puffing our way toward Canada. Finally, we got to Troy, New York, where there was a stop lasting from 15 minutes to a half-hour. I got out and called Montreal.

"You'd better be prepared," I told the league office. "I'm going to try, but I may not make it."

"You haven't missed one yet," said the man at the other end of the line. "You'll make it."

"Keep your fingers crossed," I said, hanging up.

I hopped back on the train and our trek through the snow resumed. At about seven o'clock I unpacked my overnight bag and climbed into my refereeing uniform. At about 8:20 P.M. we pulled into Montreal's Windsor Station.

I ran off the train and into the first cab I found. "Montreal Forum," I shouted at the driver, "and step on it."

The driver gave me a strange look but took off and cut through a few side streets before pulling up to the Forum on Ste. Catherine Street. At 8:28 P.M. I jumped out and walked into the Forum with my skates in my hand, completely dressed. Seven minutes later, exactly on time, I dropped the puck to start the game.

After that close call, I thought I'd faced my toughest traveling problem. But things got even more adventuresome for me after I went into broadcasting. There was, for example, the time I started out for Buffalo and wound up in Rochester, which is a nice town but didn't happen to have a NHL franchise.

Snow, again, was the problem. I had left my office early to make a Buffalo flight out of Newark Airport. But when I got to the airport, the flight was canceled. There was, however, a plane going to Rochester, which is only about 60 miles from Buffalo. That was good enough for me.

I caught the Rochester plane and arrived there about 7:00 P.M., an hour or so before the Rangers were supposed to face off against the Sabres in Buffalo. I ran outside the airport and hailed the first cab I saw. The taxi pulled up and I jumped in. When the driver asked, "Where to?" I don't think he was prepared for my answer.

"Get me to Buffalo as fast as you can," I said.

He gave me the same kind of astonished look the Montreal cabbie had when I got into his taxi with my refereeing uniform on. So I decided to add some incentive.

"It's worth $50," I said.

Needless to say, we made it. A couple of weeks later, the Rangers were back in Buffalo for another game, and naturally, it was in the middle of another snowstorm. So, of course, I wound up in Rochester again.

This time, when I got out of the terminal, there was a line of cabs waiting for this big pigeon. My driver from the last trip was at the head of the line, waving frantically and yelling, "Over here, Mr. Chadwick, over here!"

"Sorry," I shouted back. "I rented a car this time."

On another night that same winter I had just as much

trouble getting from Madison Square Garden to my home in Westbury, Long Island, as I had on my Buffalo–Rochester adventures.

Ranger goalie Gilles Villemure also lives in Westbury, and we usually ride home together on that monster of modern transportation, the Long Island Rail Road. Gilly had been out of action for a while and returned for a Sunday night game against the Chicago Black Hawks.

He was locked in a scoreless game with Chicago's Tony Esposito until late in the first period. Dennis Hull came dashing in after a loose puck and Villemure went out to meet the charge. The two players collided near the face-off circle, and Villemure went down in a heap. He had to leave the game with a sprained knee. Ed Giacomin, who was subpar himself, replaced Gilles and got blitzed with New York losing, 6-1.

After the game Villemure was hobbling around on crutches and his knee was already swelling up as we left Madison Square Garden. With us were Gilles's wife, Virginia, a Long Island girl, her parents, and Ranger statistician Art Friedman, who lives in Huntington, about 15 miles farther out on the good old Long Island Rail Road.

As soon as we left the Garden, we knew we were in trouble. An ice storm had hit the metropolitan area and the streets were glazed. Villemure could have used his goalie skates, and the rest of us might have been better off with double runners as we tiptoed our way into the LIRR station, walking as if the sidewalk was made out of eggshells.

You always climb aboard an LIRR train with a little bit of apprehension, but when it's raining ice on you, well then, the fear really grabs a hold of you. That turned out to be the perfect emotion for the situation. The LIRR run from Penn Station to Jamaica, the main stop on the way to Long Island, generally takes about 20 minutes. On this night it lasted four hours. Without lights and without heat and with one slightly groggy ex-referee, one aching goalie, and some grumbling companions.

We staggered out of the train in Jamaica, and Friedman and I made our way to the street, leaving Villemure and his swollen knee in the station with his wife and in-laws. There, miracle of miracles, we located a cab. We were ready to commandeer the vehicle but we thought we'd try diplomacy. So we half-pleaded with the cabbie to take us home.

Now the distance from Jamaica to Westbury is maybe half the haul from Rochester to Buffalo. But the cabbie hit us for a $60 fare, which was $10 more than I had paid for the ride between cities upstate. I guess the ice and the traditionally higher cost of living in New York City were the main reasons.

Since I began broadcasting, I've encountered more weather problems than I ever did as a referee. Sometimes I have weather problems that aren't entirely mine. There was the time, for example, when I plotted to beat the weatherman and wound up getting beat by him instead.

We were televising a game from Toronto on a Saturday night and I flew into town Friday night after work. Saturday was St. Patrick's Day, so I called my old Irish friend, King Clancy, to arrange for him to be interviewed between periods of the game between the Rangers and Maple Leafs.

"Sure, Bill," said Clancy. "Just don't embarrass me."

"King," I said, "you've got nothing to worry about. It would be impossible to embarrass you."

My other guest would be Denis Ball, director of the Ranger farm system, who had just returned from a scouting trip.

After lining up my interviews, I had some lunch in the Royal York Hotel and then went to my room to relax. At about three o'clock the telephone rang. It was Sal Marchiano, the play-by-play man, and he was still in New York. Marchiano, John Halligan, the Rangers' publicity director, and three writers had tried to fly to Toronto that morning and had wound up on a cook's tour of upstate New York. They had made stops in half a dozen places trying to make connections to Toronto and even tried to get a cabbie to take them there from Buffalo. But the roads were impassable, the airport was closed down, and they had run out of options.

"Bill," said Marchiano, "I'm not going to make it."

That left me with two options. I could either dump the thing in the lap of the Canadian Broadcasting Company and have the play-by-play of their "Hockey Night in Canada" broadcast fed back to New York, or I could try to do the thing myself. You know which one I chose.

I called Denis Ball immediately. "Denis," I said, "forget about our between-periods interview tonight."

Ball was puzzled. "Did you find somebody more interesting?" he needled.

"No, no," I said. "Instead of being on between periods, you're going to be on all game. You're the color man tonight. I have to do the play-by-play."

Ball was flabbergasted. He's a pretty good scout and I was a pretty good referee, but neither of us has ever been mistaken for Curt Gowdy. However, Ball is a free spirit and he'll try anything once.

"Okay," he said. "I'll do it."

I got up to the broadcast booth early that night and tried to prepare for a job I had never done before. I knew I'd have no problems identifying the Ranger players, but I had to study the Toronto numbers. With expansion, you see each team much less frequently than in the old days, and it's tough to recognize guys you only watch a couple of times a year—especially with so many of the players wearing helmets.

We went on the air at eight o'clock and I explained that because of the travel problems, Sal would not be at the game and that Denis Ball and I would be handling it. Then I said a silent prayer that we'd get a nice easy game, something like 2-1 or 3-2. The Rangers and Leafs, though, had other ideas.

Every time I looked up, it seemed, the puck was in the net. I kept shouting, "He shoots . . . he scores," so often that I almost did it a couple of times on shots that didn't go in. At the end of the first period the Rangers were leading, 4-1, and Ball was doing a terrific job with the color.

In the second period the Maple Leafs scored three goals and tied it at 4-4. Ball was much more restrained with each Toronto goal and he hardly said a word when my interview guest, King Clancy, showed up complete with green tie and shillelagh to commemorate St. Patty's Day.

My interviews with Clancy are never rehearsed. They couldn't be even if I wanted them to be. I look forward to seeing King and interviewing him because I get as much a kick out of it as I'm sure the fans do. And I'm sure King does, too. Those interviews are replays of our days together on the road, kidding and fooling around. We were two against the world at that time and we were the only two guys who believed we were right.

Ball didn't exactly enjoy Clancy's carrying-on, especially in view of Toronto's comeback in the game. And when the Leafs started scoring again in the third period, Denis clammed up tight. I don't think he said a word for the last 15 minutes, and New York lost, 7-4. The only guy happier than Denis to have the game end was the new play-by-play man.

We flew back to New York and landed at LaGuardia Airport, which would have been all right except that my car was at Kennedy. It was snowing out and I was bushed as I walked through the terminal.

"Maybe," I thought to myself, "I'll find a cab."

Now if you've ever landed at a New York airport in the middle of the night and looked for a cab to take you on something less than a $10 haul, you know it's not an easy task. I knew what I'd be up against as I waited for my bag. Just then, I felt a hand on my shoulder.

"Hey, fellow," said a soft, feminine voice, "Need a lift?"

I turned around, and there was Millie Chadwick, on hand to bail out New York's newest television personality. It reminded me of the days when I was refereeing and Millie would show up unannounced with Billy and Barbara. She was always giving me a lift, it seemed.

I was glad that I did the play-by-play in that game. It proved to me that I could do it, if I ever have to do it again. Ever since I had started sitting in the booth, I had wondered what it would be like to try to keep up with a game play-by-play-by-play. Now I know, and I'll stick to color, thank you.

14
AD LIB

I have never harbored any coaching ambitions. There are too many gray hairs in that end of hockey. But I did, inadvertently, coach a team in one game and I did it from the broadcast booth. The year was 1971, and early in the season, California was breaking in a new goalie, Gilles Meloche. The kid had shut out Boston in one of his first starts, and his next game would be at home in Oakland against the Rangers, a game Marv Albert and I were broadcasting back to New York.

Emile Francis started the game with the GAG Line—Jean Ratelle, Vic Hadfield, and Rod Gilbert. The line picked up the nickname from the initials in that phrase that described their production—Goal a Game. And they lived up to the reputation fast against Meloche. Ratelle scored in the first 15 seconds, and before the first period was over, New York had five goals and Meloche was staggering around like a punch-drunk boxer. As the teams left the ice, Albert and I discussed the Ranger barrage.

"You know, Marv," I said, "they ought to take that kid Meloche out of there. If they leave him in to take more punishment, they're liable to ruin a very good, young goalie."

Now 16 years as an NHL official had taught me not to be concernced when my advice was not heeded. I had warned my share of players that they were walking the thin line between playing and sitting in the penalty box only to have them ignore me and wind up watching instead of skating. So I hardly expected this suggestion about Meloche to be heeded.

You can imagine my surprise when at the start of the second period Lyle Carter replaced Meloche in the California goal, making Chadwick look like a soothsayer.

"Maybe," speculated Albert, "Vic Stasiuk, the coach of the Seals, is listening to our broadcast." I laughed, but Albert didn't know how close to the truth he had come. Stasiuk wasn't listening, but other people were.

Charles O. Finley, owner of the Seals, always liked to keep posted on how his team was doing. Finley was in Chicago that particular night, and one of the club's vice-presidents, Munson Campbell, was in New York relaying play-by-play of the game on a three-way phone hookup with Finley and Garry Young, the Seals' general manager, who was in Oshawa, Ontario.

When I suggested that Meloche be lifted, Campbell relayed the remark to Finley. Charley then called the Seals' dressing room and ordered his coach, Stasiuk, to change goalies. I'll bet Howard Cosell never had that fast a response to one of his ideas.

Now don't misunderstand. Not all of the suggestions I make on the air go over as well as that one did. There was, for example, the time I thought I was about to launch World War III because of some things I said to Anatoli Tarasov, the longtime coach of the Russian national team.

The Russians toured the United States for a string of exhibition games against the American Nationals a few months before the 1972 Olympic Games. One of the stops was Madison Square Garden, and the Russians stayed over in New York a couple of days and were still in town for the next Ranger home game. I figured Tarasov would be an interesting between-periods interview. There was just one hitch. Tarasov did not speak English and I certainly didn't speak Russian.

The answer, obviously, would be a translator, but the man the Russian team had been using was not available. I was kind of disappointed for a while until I realized that I had the solution to my problem right in my own family. Carl Kolon would bail me out. It was the least he could do for his father-in-law.

My daughter Barbara had married Carl, who was a graduate of the United States Naval Academy at Annapolis. He had studied Russian in school and handles the language fluently. I called Carl at the First National City Bank where he is a vice-president, and asked if he'd be interested in trying out some of his college Russian on Tarasov. He was more than happy to do it, partly because he's always ready to help out, and partly, I think, out of curiosity.

Tarasov is a roly-poly little guy who looks like a commissar. He also happens to be highly opinionated on the subject of ice hockey and I guess he was used to having his listeners nod their heads in agreement with all of his thoughts on the game. I think he was surprised when I replied, through Carl, with a few *"nyets."* I, you see, am also rather opinionated about this game.

Pretty soon, Carl was sitting between two characters who were hollering at each other in no uncertain terms. I needled Tarasov about the Russians not hitting and he gave it back to me about the violence of the NHL. I questioned the checkerboard passing style used by the Russians and he argued that it demonstrated the total control of their game by his players. Meanwhile, my son-in-law was bobbing back and forth like a guy at a tennis match, all the time being very careful to soften each translation so we wouldn't get thrown off the air or, worse than that, start an international incident. I have enough problems without getting the State Department on my neck about not being polite to a visitor from a foreign nation—especially from Russia. I think Carl had a good time with us, because I had trouble getting the mike back from him.

I had run into the language barrier before. On the ice more than one French player has used his native tongue to ream me out. Then there was my interview with Marcel Pelletier, an old goalie who now serves as player personnel director of the Philadelphia Flyers. Pelletier's effectiveness in the front office has been reflected by Philadelphia's success on the ice. He's not only a good evaluator of hockey talent but he also has a good sense of humor.

We were televising a game from Philadelphia when I invited Pelletier to come on between the first and second periods. "Sure, I do it, Bill," he said. "I need some more shirts," referring to the gifts we give interview guests. "You know," he added, "some of our extra guys don't get much ice time, but they are the best dressers on the team because of those interviews with you radio and TV people."

I'm always nervous about every interview I do for a number of reasons. Let's face it, I'm no professional broadcaster. Give me a whistle and I can handle myself with no trouble. Give me a mike and I'll give it my best shot, but I can't guarantee the outcome.

Well, the first period ended and I looked around nervously, trying to spot Pelletier. That, of course, is the first problem—making sure your guest arrives for the interview. There, off behind a camera, was Pelletier. "Thank goodness," I invariably say to myself when a guest shows up at the appointed time and place.

I did a 60-second recap of the first period, and then we broke for a commercial. While we were off the air, I waved for Pelletier to sit down next to me on camera. Marcel stepped in, smiling.

"Okay, Marcel," I said, "we'll talk first about the success of the Flyers and how you found these players. Then we can talk about the first period."

"Fine, Bill," said Pelletier, nodding.

Now the director gave me my cue. "Ten seconds . . . five seconds . . . air."

"My guest between the first and second periods here in the Spectrum in Philadelphia," I began, "is Marcel Pelletier, player personnel director of the Flyers. Welcome, Marcel." I turned to Pelletier, and I immediately knew from the devilish look in Marcel's eye that I was in trouble.

"Ah, *bonjour,* Bill," answered Pelletier. *"Comment 'allez vous? C'est une jeu excitant, n'est-ce pas?"*

Marcel was babbling in French to me, and I don't speak that language any better than I do Russian. I gaped at the old goalie and I would have been furious if the scene hadn't been so funny. Pelletier's eyes were positively dancing, and the TV crew was doubled over in laughter. They had set me up and I had really been taken. If I'd had a whistle, I would have gotten rid of all of them on the spot.

The behind-the-scenes broadcast crew has had its fun with me more than once. For a while we carried a feature in which we asked listeners to send in questions that I would answer between periods. A couple of months after the series began, we got a letter asking who had scored the first goal in the new Madison Square Garden.

Well, I've seen my share of goals scored, and after a while, they all seem to run together. For the moment, I honestly couldn't remember who had gotten the first goal. I stalled for time, remembering that the game was between the Rangers and Philadelphia. Mentally, I tried to picture the goal, but I was coming up with a blank. Then I got bailed out—or at least I thought I was—when one of the crew members passed me a slip of paper. On it was written two words. "Gary Dornhoefer," it said.

"Oh, yes," I ad-libbed. "The first goal in the new Garden. Sure, I remember that one," I fibbed. "That was Gary Dornhoefer of the Philadelphia Flyers."

Well, I had the team right but the player wrong. It was Philadelphia's goal all right, but the guy who scored it was Wayne Hicks. And I found out fast that plenty of hockey fans remembered the goal, even if I didn't. My mailbag was overrun with letters correcting my boo-boo. Some of them were strongly worded, almost as strongly worded as some of the criticism my refereeing sometimes stimulated. I corrected my mistake on the next broadcast, and it was the last time I accepted any help with my answers.

When I was a referee, I called plays just the way I saw them and now that I'm a broadcaster, I haven't changed that policy one bit. Some people think I'm outspoken, but I can't help that. There's no changing Bill Chadwick at this stage of the game.

I'm honest, and sometimes that honesty gets me in trouble. There was a time when it also caused a player boycott against me. I had made a crack on the air about a Ranger player who just didn't seem to be playing up to his capabilities. A day or two later, Vic Hadfield, captain of the Rangers, came to talk to me about some of the players being disturbed over the remarks I had been making on television. Vic said that the guy I had said wasn't producing as well as I thought he should had told him that his wife and kids had heard my comment on television. The kids burst into tears over it and his wife was all upset.

"Look, Vic," I said. "The way I work, I have to be honest in my comments. In the same vein, while I may criticize once in a while, if a player plays well, I'm the first to compliment him. And if a player can take applause, he must be able to take criticism."

Unfortunately, this didn't sit well with Hadfield, and for the next couple of weeks, every time I asked a player to come on between periods, I was turned down. Pretty soon I got the message. The players were boycotting me. Finally, we got to Detroit and Vic and I arranged a private meeting. We hashed the whole thing out, and I think afterward Hadfield understood my position. Things were all right after that and it was the only time I have ever been penalized for my criticism of the Rangers.

I guess I've never been harder on any Ranger player than I was on Gene Carr. Now Carr can skate like the wind, and that's half the battle to making it in the National Hockey League. I think it was his speed more than anything else that convinced Emile Francis to trade three players to St. Louis for Carr.

Gene had been the fourth player chosen in the 1971 amateur draft of graduating junior players. He had some pretty good company in that draft. Guy Lafleur, Marcel Dionne, and Jocelyn Guevremont were the only players chosen ahead of him. Some of those picked behind him were Rick Martin, Steve Vickers, and Rick Kehoe. All of them have progressed farther and faster than Gene Carr.

After the Rangers acquired Carr, he invariably would let his speed take him right out of a play. Playing left wing on a line with Walt Tkaczuk and Bill Fairbairn, Carr was getting all sorts of excellent scoring opportunities. And he was blowing most of them. Finally, with the frustration any Ranger fan felt—and I don't deny that I root for the Rangers nowadays—I rapped Gene Carr. "He couldn't put the puck in the ocean if he was standing on the end of a dock," I said.

It didn't take long for that remark to get back to Gene Carr. A week later he scored three goals in a single game—his first NHL hat trick. As reporters bunched around him in the Ranger dressing room, Carr decided to get even with The Big Whistle. "I guess," he said, "it's a pretty big ocean, eh?"

I must give Carr credit, though. He never voiced any objection to me about that crack. I had conversations with him about it and I told him that I felt my statement, while it was controversial, made Gene a more popular player in New

York. People took sides. Either they'd be with Carr against The Big Whistle or against Carr and agreeing with The Big Whistle. So I think in the long run it helped Carr. And there's no one who wants Gene to succeed more than I do even though he's with the Los Angeles Kings.

When I first started broadcasting, I made some ground rules for myself. First of all, I always interview the people from the visiting team first. That's because the history of hockey shows that the home team tends to get stronger as the game goes on. The visiting team is likely to be in the game after one period but could be out of it after two. And a general manager is going to be more talkative when his club is in a close game than he will be if his team is being blown out of the building. You have a better chance to get positive answers and cooperation from a visiting team after the first period than you do after the second.

When I started broadcasting nobody gave me a book on how to interview guests. Oh, sure, Marv Albert and Sal Marchiano and Jim Gordon all offered some very good advice, but really I was pretty much on my own. I don't think that was so very bad. I believe that every interviewer has his own style, and if you ever tried to run a conversation along structured rules, you'd really lay an egg. A hockey game can be run by rules. An interview can't. It all comes off the top of your head. You get spontaneous, impromptu answers, and that's a lot better than something that's been rehearsed.

I've always prided myself on my honesty, both on the ice and behind the microphone. But sometimes, it can backfire. In the first round of the 1973 Stanley Cup playoffs, for example, the Rangers upset Boston and eliminated the East Division champions in only five games. It was an exciting victory and I was caught up in it completely. When it became obvious that the Rangers were about to win the clinching game, I went on the air and announced the team's return plans to New York that night. We were landing at LaGuardia Airport and I figured that a little welcoming committee would do the players' spirit some good. I never expected 5,000 fans in that committee.

Our plane was diverted from its planned terminal but that didn't fool the fans. They overran the runway and stormed the plane. There were very few police there, and for a while it was a frightening scene—all of it caused by The Big Whistle. I had to do something, so I grabbed a bullhorn from one of the policemen.

"Please," I shouted into the horn, "stay back. Let the players out. Please. You're here because of me. Do a favor for me and let them out. Please."

How we ever got out of there in one piece I'll never know. Ed Giacomin's car was nearly overturned, and it was a frightening episode. Shortly afterward Emile Francis sent around a memo directing that the team's itinerary no longer be announced.

I laughed when I got it. "Don't worry," I said, remembering the airport scene, "it'll never happen again."

15

PUCK LUCK

Once upon a time, there were six big league hockey teams and players would damn near cut off their right arms for an opportunity to play with one of them. But those days are gone forever. They ended back in 1967 when the National Hockey League launched the most ambitious expansion program in the history of sports. You hear a lot of static about that expansion program even now, nearly a decade later. Old-timers yearn for the time when hockey's western outpost was Chicago. But I don't happen to be one of those old-timers.

When I started refereeing there were seven NHL teams. That was in 1939. When I hung up my skates for the last time, there were six teams, the poverty-stricken New York Americans being the only dropout. That's not much of a change in 16 seasons. All around the NHL, other sports were expanding. Football, baseball, and basketball all added new franchises in new cities—new places to sell their game. But the NHL bided its time until 1967. Then it moved, not into one or two new markets, but into a half dozen of them, doubling the league from 6 to 12 teams.

The new clubs were the Philadelphia Flyers, Minnesota North Stars, St. Louis Blues, Pittsburgh Penguins, Los Angeles Kings, and Oakland Seals. They were placed in their own division which insured that in their first year, one of those new teams would finish in first place. The New York Rangers haven't done that in 32 years.

In 1970 two more teams were added—the Buffalo Sabres and Vancouver Canucks. Then, in 1972 came the Atlanta Flames and—a stone's throw from my house in Westbury, Long Island (provided you have a good arm)—the New York Islanders. For 1974-1975 Kansas City and Washington were added, bringing NHL membership from 6 teams in 1967 to 18 teams only seven years later.

Some people say it was too much too soon. They argue that there just isn't enough hockey talent around to stock all those new teams. And, of course, the development of the rival World Hockey Association with a dozen or so teams of its own has also sapped the player market.

Well, I watched hockey in the old six-team years and I watch it now. I'm not going to deny that the caliber of play has been diluted. As my friend Clarence Campbell says so often, "You can't take a bottle of scotch and split it into two bottles, each half filled with water, and expect to have the same strength drink." But for me, the half-scotch tastes pretty good, too.

The game is still pleasing to watch and that's proven by the attendance records that the NHL sets every year. You can't buy a ticket in a lot of rinks around the league. They play to capacity crowds in Chicago today—with kids like Darcy Rota and John Marks skating for the Black Hawks— just as often as they did when old pros like Bobby Hull and Pat Stapleton were playing. To me, that's a tremendous endorsement. People will come out to watch this game no matter who's playing it. Check out a suburban rink early some morning when a couple of teams of kid hockey players are going at each other. The joint will be rocking with people hollering every bit as loud as if they were watching hockey's biggest stars playing. This is just an exciting game no matter who's playing it.

The difference in the NHL today is you don't have as close a group of solid hockey players as you had when there were only six teams. The talent, obviously, has been spread out. In the old days, every team had a superstar. Today, that's no longer true. Oh, sure, there's a Phil Esposito and a Bobby Orr and an Yvan Cournoyer and others. But these guys are the exceptions, not the rules. The day of the superstar—that is the superstar on every team—is gone, in my opinion.

When the NHL expanded the first time, the pet word you heard all the time around the league was "parity." That was what Campbell and the other officials were striving for—a condition where old teams would be on an equal footing with new ones. Well, it's taken a few years to produce that parity, but I think the NHL has reached it because of the universal amateur draft.

In the old days teams could lock up a good young prospect when he was barely a teen-ager. Bobby Orr was in the Bruins' camp from the time he was 14 years old. But that can't happen anymore. Under Campbell's leadership the NHL has established a universal amateur draft that allows all teams an equal opportunity at the top junior players when they turn 20 years of age.

The only thing now that can make one organization better than another over the long haul is their own scouting systems and evaluations of amateur players. The Philadelphia Flyers, for example, came up with a superstar in Bobby Clarke, but he was available to all 11 other teams when he was drafted in 1969. The Flyers saw something in him the others did not, and it paid off for them. His success is a credit to them and the draft system.

Teams can't pick and control the players they want anymore, but they can still find hockey players that might not be rated as high in other teams' evaluations. It's all a matter of organization. That makes success today an even tougher achievement than it was when all you had to do was outbid five other clubs for a promising young player. Now you have to outscout and outguess 17 other teams.

I guess Clarke impresses me as much as any other player in the league today. He is a marvelous center and his development to star status coincides with the climb of the Philadelphia Flyers in the NHL's West Division. I think the thing that impresses me most about this young man is the knowledge that he has climbed to superstar status despite being a diabetic.

Clarke requires frequent insulin shots, and the Flyers' trainer carries special supplies along for application to Bobby in case of an emergency. Clarke doesn't like to talk about his ailment or to have others discuss it in relation to his hockey ability. But the fact remains that he has succeeded in a very rugged sport despite a disability that might have sidetracked others.

I supposed that subconsciously my own handicap increases my admiration for Clarke. I remember people saying that a man with sight in only one eye couldn't referee. They're probably the same people who said a kid with diabetes couldn't succeed in the NHL.

Clarke is only one of several outstanding centers around the NHL today. In Boston they tell you that Phil Esposito is the greatest thing since beans. And you know, I'm tempted to agree.

Esposito, of course, is the NHL's perennial scoring champion. He won the scoring title for the fifth time in the last six years in 1974 and grinds out points and goals like a machine.

Phil started his NHL career with the Chicago Black Hawks but really came into his own when he was traded to

Boston in a deal that the Black Hawks still regret today. It's no coincidence either that the Bruins became winners the year they acquired Esposito, Ken Hodge, and Fred Stanfield from Chicago for Gilles Marotte, Pit Martin, and Jack Norris.

At Chicago, Esposito played under the shadow of Bobby Hull. Phil centered for Hull and it's kind of tough to achieve your own identity when your left wing is one of the greatest scorers in the history of hockey. When he got to Boston, Phil discovered the slot position—that area just in front of the net—and decided that would be the perfect place to set up permanent housekeeping. He lives there and it enables him to pick up an awful lot of goals. Some critics call them garbage goals, but they count just as much as one of those 50-foot slap shots.

His size is a tremendous asset for Esposito. He's so big and strong that it's all but impossible to oust him from in front of that net. All of the players today seem bigger than they were when I came into the NHL. And Esposito is one of the biggest and certainly one of the strongest.

It's a funny thing, but the Bruins have a guy playing on Esposito's right side who is in the same shadow with Phil now as Phil was when he played in Chicago with Bobby Hull. I'm referring to Ken Hodge, who, like Espo, is a big strong kid with a good scoring touch.

Hodge digs for the puck and that's something I've always admired in a hockey player. What's more, he asserts himself and has a good hard shot. Whose rebounds do you think Esposito is forever scooping into the net? Hodge is the guy who is doing a lot of the work on all those goals Phil scores.

Then there is a fellow in Boston who wears number 4. That's all the introduction Bobby Orr needs. Ted Green once said that Orr has 18 speeds and I think that might be underestimating him.

It isn't only his speed that makes Orr so spectacular. It's his deceptiveness. He's like a gear-shift car. He can shift speeds whenever he wants and that's an awesome weapon for a hockey player to have. You think he's going all out when all of a sudden he comes up with that little extra spurt just when he needs it.

I think Orr has reached the point now where he paces himself. He does not go all out all the time. He's certainly a much better hockey player today than he's ever been before because of that deceptiveness. He waits until the opportunity presents itself and then cuts loose.

Having Esposito and Orr on the same team together gives Boston a tremendous offensive punch. I think they complement each other. I don't think one depends upon the other, but together they make the Bruins overpowering.

Over in Montreal, the Canadiens have a right wing who shoots left and scores a lot of goals. That sounds like a description of Maurice Richard. A lot of people compare Yvan Cournoyer with the Rocket. Don't include me in that group, though.

In no way, shape, or form would I compare Cournoyer with the Rocket. Cournoyer is certainly a much faster skater than the Rocket, but there is nobody, in my opinion, including Cournoyer, in the game today who has the desire or the flair to get a goal the way the Rocket did. Richard was just out of this world when it came to getting the puck and going for the net.

Cournoyer is not deceptive in any way. He just has tremendous speed and he knows where the net is. In that respect, I guess, he does resemble the Rocket. But if I needed one goal and I could pick any Montreal player in history to try for it, my man would be Richard, not Cournoyer.

There's another Canadien who has been somewhat overshadowed by Cournoyer. That would be Frank Mahovlich, who started his career with Toronto and has also played for Detroit. Mahovlich has had a fantastic career with more than 500 goals in the National Hockey League.

He was one of the first players to come up with the real hard shot. And he had some spectacular scoring years while he was with the Maple Leafs. He was so impressive that Chicago Black Hawk's owner Jim Norris once offered Toronto $1 million for him. Now the Norris I remember didn't throw that kind of money around haphazardly. So you know that Mahovlich must have been a pretty fair hockey player to command that kind of an offer.

Frank is a deceptive skater. He takes long strides and moves up and down the rink in a hurry with minimum of effort. He is such a fluid skater and seems so nonchalant on the ice that people used to accuse him of loafing. But he's no loafer. He just gets the job done a lot more easily than other guys because he's more talented.

For many years, while I was in the league and after I retired, the New York Rangers were a rag-tag outfit. They stayed that way until the mid-sixties, when Emile Francis came along and rebuilt the club from top to bottom. A key part of that rebuilding was the assembly of the so-called GAG Line consisting of center Jean Ratelle and his wingers, Rod Gilbert and Vic Hadfield.

Putting those three guys together was a stroke of genius. Ratelle is a superb playmaker, Hadfield works hard in the corners, and Gilbert has a knack for getting free in front of the net. The rise of the Rangers can be traced to the success of this trio.

Unfortunately, injuries have hampered the line. Their effectiveness has been greatly reduced because their success depends in just about equal amounts on all three of them. In the 1971–1972 season there wasn't a finer line in hockey. Then Ratelle broke his ankle in the final month of the season and missed the last 15 games. He still scored more than 100 points that season, but that injury cost him some of his speed. Since the injury, Jean's performance has fallen off.

Then Hadfield was plagued by a whole string of injuries. First he broke his thumb in a fight when he conked some other guy who had a head as hard as a helmet. Then he bruised his other hand, and he never really healed. But the scariest injury of all came when he was hit in the face by a shot and suffered a concussion. He was out for some time with that one and never was quite right after that.

Those accidents turned things around on Hadfield. Vic just isn't a very good hockey player when he's thinking of injuries, and it seems to me that Vic is a little more concerned about himself; and once you play that way, you're just not as effective.

Gilbert, on the other hand, has become more effective. I think Rod is a better hockey player now than he has been at any time since he came up to the Rangers in 1961. He's doing more things now, and he has reached the potential that everybody in the NHL always thought he possessed. Rod passed Andy Bathgate, the former Ranger great, and is the highest scorer in club history.

On defense, the Rangers' answer to Bobby Orr is Brad Park, a great player who would receive considerably more publicity if Orr was not in the league. Brad plays in Orr's shadow and I think this has affected Park. After all, if it were not for Orr, Brad would probably be considered the best defenseman in the league.

It seems to me, though, that Brad could be more consistent. He'll have two or three great hockey games and then he seems to lose his desire. A player endowed with so much talent shouldn't have those letdowns.

My favorite player to watch when I get to see Chicago is Stan Mikita. I believe, without any reservation, that he is one of the four or five very best centers ever to play in the NHL. He certainly is the best face-off man in the league today and is an absolute wizard with that hockey stick.

Mikita has enjoyed a fantastic career. Here's a man who came into the league as a tough hockey player who led the NHL in penalties. He found out that wasn't the way to play hockey, so the next year he turned right around and won the Lady Byng Trophy, emblematic of clean play. He's the heart and soul of the Chicago hockey club.

Chicago also has a pretty good left-winger named Hull. No, not Bobby, but his brother Dennis. Like Phil Esposito and Mikita, Dennis played in Bobby Hull's shadow for a long time with Chicago and his ability wasn't fully appreciated until Bobby transferred to the World Hockey·Association. I think the best thing that ever happened to Dennis Hull was his brother leaving the team.

When Bobby Hull played with the Black Hawks, the team wasn't really as successful as it has been since he left. That's no rap at Bobby, who is a super hockey player, but the fact is that he felt he had to carry the club on his back. So Bobby would get 50 goals and nobody else on the team would get 20. That kind of hockey doesn't make for championships.

I think the Black Hawks turned the corner when Pit Martin popped off during training camp one year, calling the team individualistic and rapping some of the superstars—Bobby included—who played only in the offensive zone and forgot all about their defensive responsibilities.

In retrospect, I think Martin's remarks made Bobby Hull a better competitor. He became more of a complete hockey player. I'm sure when he stepped into a coaching role with Winnipeg of the World Hockey Association, he appreciated even more the defensive aspects of this game, and players who work as hard in their own zone as they do when they're on the other team's end of the ice.

The Black Hawks' goalie is Tony Esposito, whose style I don't think I'll ever figure out. He looks like he's so easy to beat that Aunt Emma could score against him. Yet game after game, season after season, he turns in topnotch netminding for the Black Hawks.

When I first saw Esposito, I have to admit I didn't think
he'd last a month in the NHL. He looks awkward and leaves
all kinds of openings for shooters. But it's a case of now you
see it, now you don't. Espo will show you a big piece of the net
and when you shoot for it, all of a sudden, he's got the area
covered. I don't know how the man does it.

He's an unorthodox goalie but he seems to get himself in
the way of an awful lot of shots. You keep waiting for him to
make a mistake and for that cockeyed style of his to betray
him. But it never happens and he keeps getting better and
better. I have a lot of respect for him and I'd have to admit
that I misjudged his ability. But I still don't understand how
he does it.

You'd have to say—and the statistics bear this out—that
Esposito is one of the best goalies in the league over the last
half-dozen years or so. Another one would be Ken Dryden,
who led Montreal to the Stanley Cup in two of the three
seasons he played with the Canadiens before sitting out
1973-1974 to fulfill his law internship.

Dryden, too, is more or less unorthodox and sometimes
he looks like a great big giraffe in the net. But he keeps the
puck out and that's what goaltending is all about.

The Rangers' Eddie Giacomin also has to be classed near
the top of modern-day goalies. Giacomin is a workhorse who
seems to play better when he's used a lot. He's good with his
stick and that always helps a goalie. He's also a lot more conventional than either Esposito or Dryden and that sits particularly well with the staid old Big Whistle.

I don't need to say that the present game of hockey is
quite different from the one I used to referee. The red line
opened the game up considerably. Just about every rink today
is the standard 200 feet long and 85 feet wide and that has
made it a more uniform game. Teams and owners today are
more anxious to give a show and improve the image of the
game. Years ago, the owners were a bunch of egotists who
were only interested in their own images and didn't give a hoot

about hockey. It was like having six Charley Finleys running the clubs.

One thing that hasn't changed, though, is that precious commodity called puck luck. Good players have always had it. The puck seems to follow the top players around. They don't have to go after it. It's like a magnet. That's because, when you're a good hockey player, you have the instinct that tells you where the puck is going to be. It looks like the puck is coming to you, but it's not really. That's the difference between the great hockey players and the mediocre ones.

When I refereed in the National Hockey League, there were, as I have said, only six big league teams. And it stayed that way for more than a decade after I retired. Then came expansion and with it, a brand new league, the World Hockey Association, with 12 franchises of its own stretching into cities like Edmonton, Houston, and a few other spots that had never seen big league hockey. I'm not sure that what the WHA offered was exactly big league, though.

The WHA arrived on the scene in 1972, five years after the initial NHL expansion. And when it did, those original NHL expansion teams were still experiencing problems finding major league players to stock their rosters. The addition of 12 more teams simply diluted the product even more.

On the other hand, the new league offered more job opportunities in hockey for everyone associated with the game. So even though the quality of hockey wasn't the very best, the development of the new league did have some advantages. But even with Bobby Hull, Gerry Cheevers, and Gordie Howe skating in the WHA, the new league generally doesn't compare with the kind of hockey played in the top minors like the American and Western leagues in pre-expansion days.

Salaries, of course, are another of the major changes we've seen in hockey. I've always believed that a player has to be hungry to be good. Being hungry feeds desire, and desire makes an athlete give that little bit extra. I think players with big salaries are subconsciously not going to take chances with their futures. You just don't have that gung ho atmosphere today that was prevalent when I was refereeing. This has happened in all sports. We all think differently today, I guess.

Here's an example of how the economics of hockey have changed: When I started in the NHL, I had a per diem allowance of $8. That $8 was supposed to cover food, hotels, taxis, and any other expenses I might incur. Of course, that was only for my first four or five years in the league. After that, I went up—to $10. Today, when I travel with the Rangers, I get $20 a day for food alone.

Money wasn't terribly important to me, though. I was proud of being a referee and I worked hard to be the very best ref I could be. It tickles me when people remember me that way. Being on television with the Rangers has naturally increased my exposure, and a lot of kids who never saw me call a penalty stop me in the street to say hello to The Big Whistle. But it's the guy who says, "You're the referee," who makes me proudest.

I believe I was a good referee because of my eye, not in spite of it. I had always felt I had to work a little harder because I only had the one eye. It never entered my mind in those days, but as I think back now, I remember that I was always on top of the play, always closer than the others. I think it made me a better referee. And I think being a referee made me a better broadcaster.

I know one thing. It has been a lot safer for me in the booth than on the ice. People don't throw things at you up there.

INDEX